SQUASH

Rachel Bard and Caroline Kellogg

Drawings by Rik Olson

101 Productions
San Francisco

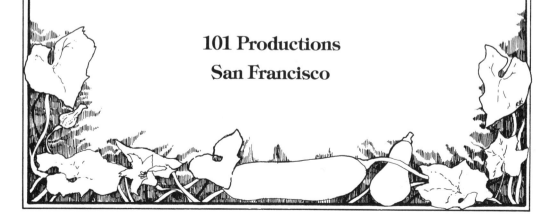

Printed and bound in the United States of America

Distributed to the book trade in the United States
by Charles Scribner's Sons, New York, and in Canada
by Van Nostrand Reinhold Ltd., Toronto

Published by 101 Productions
834 Mission Street
San Francisco, California 94103

Library of Congress Cataloging in Publication Data

Bard, Rachel
    Squash.

    (Edible garden series)
    Includes index.
    1. Cookery (Squash)   2. Squash. I. Kellogg,
Caroline   joint author.   II. Title.   III. Se-
ries.
TX803.S67B36   641.6'5'62   77-3917
ISBN 0-89286-113-4

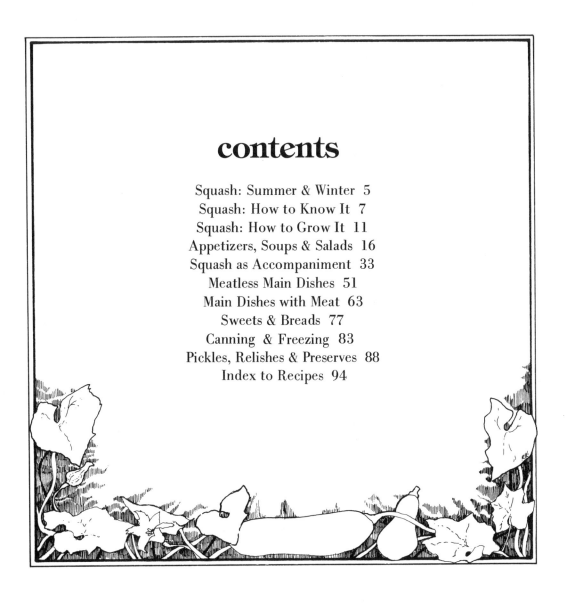

contents

squash: summer & winter

Squash, as every good cook knows, has a split personality. There are summer squash and winter squash. Though the plants are nearly identical and grow under the same conditions, their products are as different as summer and winter themselves.

Summer squash are prodigals, meant to be enjoyed with abandon while the sun shines. They don't store well for very long, and are best when very fresh—within minutes from being cut from the vine, if possible.

Winter squash encourage one's provident, plan-ahead tendencies. They are harvested much later, and thriftily stored so you can savor their hearty golden goodness all through the dark fall and winter months.

Both kinds are prolific and versatile. Anyone who has ever planted even a couple of hills of zucchini or Hubbard has been forced to experiment with new ways to use the abundant fruits of his labors. Collecting recipes gets to be a necessary and rewarding game. (Which is how this book came about. After years of growing squash and devising ways to cook it, we wanted to share our pleasure in the squash game.)

As for versatility, squash can be baked, sautéed, marinated, stuffed, braised, steamed, fried, scalloped, mashed, pickled, frozen. You can use squash in bread, soup, relishes, cookies, muffins, puddings, pies. It can be served as an appetizer, added to an omelet, fried as a fritter, incorporated in a hamburger. It can be served hot or cold. Even the squash blossom is edible, indeed a delicacy, when dipped in batter and deep-fried.

Besides being so versatile, squash is one of the easiest and least bothersome vegetables to grow. A few seeds will keep a family well supplied for a year. If you can't grow your own, nowadays you'll find squash—in great variety—in the market the year around. And it is one of the most reasonably priced vegetables.

Nutritionally, it's tops. Both green and yellow squash are good sources of vitamin A. For low-calorie diets, the summer squash are ideal. And winter squash are excellent sources of easy-to-digest carbohydrate.

All in all, if we were to designate a national vegetable, this would be it. The botanical name is *Cucurbita*—derived from the Latin for gourd. But squash as a culinary vegetable is definitely native to the New World. It was a staple of the American Indians' diet long before the white man came and followed their good example.

Squash was on the first Thanksgiving Day menu, just as it is traditionally on many today. The very name bespeaks the indigenous origin: squash is short for *isquoutersquash,* from the Algonquin and Massachusetts Indian languages.

Despite all these virtues, squash is not used to its full potential. One reason may be the lack, up to now, of a comprehensive collection of recipes, a lack this book hopes to fill.

But another reason may be that many cooks are hampered by unfamiliarity with the wide number of varieties and shapes. And, to add to the confusion, the same variety is often known by different names. So here is a simplified guide.

squash: how to know it

SUMMER SQUASH

These should be harvested while young and tender. If caught young, most may be eaten in their entirety—seeds, skin and all.

In most of the zucchini recipes in this book, other types of summer squash may be substituted, especially the other green varieties (cocozelle, caserta).

Caserta Dark green-yellowish skin, 7 to 8 inches long, with white-yellow flesh. Similar to cocozelle (see below). Usually in the market all year.

Cocozelle Smooth-skinned, dark green with paler green stripes. Looks and tastes much like zucchini. Green-white flesh.

Chayote (chä-yō-tä) Related to squash, but more generally regarded as an edible gourd. Shaped somewhat like a pear and about the size of acorn squash, with pale green, irregularly furrowed skin. When young, may be cooked without peeling. One large seed in center, edible.

Courgette British term for vegetable marrows which are picked when very young.

Cymling (sim-ling) Also called pattypan, bush, scallop or white summer squash. Small, round, pie-shaped, with a scalloped edge. Green when young, white when mature. Thin-skinned when small; if it gets big, may need peeling.

Vegetable marrow (British) Refers to zucchini or cocozelle.

Yellow or golden crookneck and yellow straightneck Both have yellow skin, slightly warted on crookneck and smoother on straightneck. Crookneck curves at its slender neck, straightneck is shaped somewhat like a zucchini. Both should be harvested young so the shell does not develop a tough skin.

Zucchini Best when dark green, bright and shiny, 4 to 10 inches long, and when squash feels heavy for its size. Most versatile of squash, zucchini can be served raw or cooked, alone or with other ingredients; can be frozen or preserved. It is the easiest of the summer squash to grow.

WINTER SQUASH

Winter squash should be eaten when fully mature. On most, the skin is hard and thick and is not usually eaten. The butternut is the only winter squash with a thin skin. The seeds of these squash, especially thin-skinned ones like those of the butternut, can be eaten when dried. When recipes in this book call for winter squash, any of the following may be used.

Acorn Known also as Danish, Des Moines or table queen, this squash is dark green, smooth, corrugated. A smallish squash, it has tender, orange flesh with a large seed cavity. Ideal for stuffing.

Banana Quite often long, up to 18 or 24 inches, and shaped like a big frankfurter. Pale orange-cream skin. Fine-textured flesh is orange colored and seed cavity is large. Often sold cut in sections.

Buttercup Sometimes called turban, for its shape. Whitish, round top; squat, round body of dark green with faint gray stripes. Skin is thinner than most winter squash. It has orange flesh and is one of the sweetest of the squash.

Butternut Largish, creamy pinkish, smooth-skinned squash, shaped somewhat like an enormous peanut. Flesh is fine-grained, yellow-orange, considered finest-flavored by many.

Delicata Rather small oval squash with green-and-yellow- striped skin. May be cooked like acorn.

Delicious Large, shaped like a top with ridges. Available as golden or green type. Light orangish-gold flesh.

Gold Nugget Hard-skinned, large as a cantaloupe, looks something like a small golden pumpkin. Free-from-fiber orange flesh, with a nutty flavor.

Hubbard Globular, tapering at both ends. Skin is ridged and warty, dark green or orangy. If the former, sometimes called Blue Hubbard, which grows very large. If the latter, Golden Hubbard. Flesh is thick, orange and sweet. May grow to several hundred pounds, as county fair visitors know. In the market, is usually sold cut into sections.

8

Marblehead Large round or oval-shaped squash with very hard, gray-green warty skin and yellow-orange flesh.

Pumpkin Also a member of the *Cucurbita* family; main differences from squash are in the structural differences of the stems (squash stems are cylindrical and soft at maturity, while pumpkin stems are five-sided, deeply grooved and very woody), and in the very limited common association of pumpkin with pie and jack-o'-lanterns. But just as winter squash can be used to make a "pumpkin" pie, so can pumpkin be used for nearly every recipe in this book calling for winter squash.

Spaghetti Oval-shaped, white to golden, 8 to 12 inches long. Flesh is pale yellow and when cooked forms strands which look like spaghetti but taste like squash.

SEASONS FOR BUYING SQUASH IN THE MARKET

Of the most popular summer squash, zucchini and caserta are generally in the market the year around. Yellow crookneck, yellow straightneck and cymlings are in the market summer and fall.

Of the winter varieties, Hubbard and butternut are in the market fall and winter. Acorn is generally available year-round. Marblehead and Gold Nugget are available fall through March. Buttercup is in the market in late summer. Banana is available from August through March; Delicata from September through November.

CHOOSING SQUASH IN THE MARKET

The skin of summer squash should be soft; a hard skin means squash are too ripe. Select summer squash that are firm, not wrinkled or shriveled, with unblemished skin and no soft spots. Zucchini should be bright green, shiny, firm, heavy for their size. Cymlings should be small, pale green, unbruised. The older they get, the whiter and harder the skin and less flavorful the flesh. Yellow crookneck and straightneck also develop hard skin if allowed to grow more than about 8 inches long.

Since winter squash keep well, your chances of getting a bad one in the grocery store are minimal, but make sure they are hard and firm and without any soft spots.

SIZES

Use 2-1/2 pounds of winter squash for 4 servings, and 1-1/2 pounds of summer squash for 4 servings. When recipes in this book refer to sizes of squash, use these guides.

Zucchini

    small (4 to 6 inches in length) = 1/4 pound

    medium (7 inches in length) = 1/2 pound

    large (10 to 12 inches in length) = 3/4 to 1 pound

Cymling

    small (2-1/2 inches in diameter) = 3 to 4 ounces

    medium (3-1/2 to 4 inches) = 5 to 6 ounces

Butternut

    small (8-1/2 to 9 inches in length) = 2 pounds

    large (12 to 14 inches in length) = 4-1/2 pounds

Acorn

    small (5 to 6 inches in length) = 1 pound

    large (7 to 8 inches in length) = 1-1/2 to 1-3/4 pounds

Yellow crookneck

    small (5 inches in length) = up to 1/4 pound

    large (7 inches in length) = 7 to 8 ounces

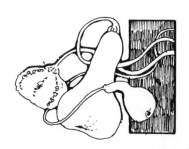

Three pounds of winter squash, when cooked and puréed, make 3-3/4 cups; a medium summer squash makes about 2 cups grated or chopped squash.

squash: how to grow it

No matter how limited your garden, you can still grow a good squash crop. Summer varieties are bushy and take less space than winter. If you are a deck or patio gardener, and have a large planter or tub, you may, with one or two plants, produce enough summer squash to keep you happy for months. Winter squash, with its longer vines, needs more spreading-out space. But it is so nutritional that only a few plants will contribute to good health. Also, watch for new dwarf varieties, such as the bush acorn that takes only about 4 feet of space.

Preparation of soil All squash like ample full sun. Choose an area with fairly light rich soil with good drainage. You may plant in "hills" (seed sown in circle) or rows.

If the former, for each hill dig a hole about 18 inches deep and 18 inches square. You will need to cultivate only the soil within this basin, since this is all the space the roots can use. Spade the soil thoroughly to break up clods and turn under existing weeds. Gradually incorporate organic matter such as compost, well-rotted manure or peat moss into the soil. Locate hills 4 feet apart for summer squash, 6 to 8 feet apart for winter squash. Many gardeners raise the hills 3 or 4 inches higher than the level of the rest of the garden for faster results where soil is colder. This can be done by incorporating more loam and composted matter into the soil to increase the volume.

Also, you might try growing your squash on a compost heap, which gives it the advantages of a raised hill and plenty of nutrients. To quote from L. H. Bailey's much-respected *Cyclopedia of Horticulture*, squash will grow on a rubbish-heap "with wonderful vigor, and fruit abundantly."

If you plant in rows, you need to prepare an 18-inch-deep, 18-inch-wide strip of soil for each row. Leave 3 feet between rows for summer squash, 5 feet for winter. Again, work soil until it is loose and without clods. Spade in wood chips, peat moss or aged sawdust, and rotted manure.

11

How to plant Plant summer squash seeds 1 inch deep and winter squash 1 to 1-1/2 inches deep. Allow plenty of space between plants. In hills, sow 6 to 8 seeds per hill to be sure of 3 to 5 plants per hill after thinning, for both summer and winter squash. If you plant in rows, allow 2 to 2-1/2 feet between summer squash plants after thinning, 3 to 4 feet between winter squash plants after thinning.

You may, of course, buy already started plants or start your own indoors or in a greenhouse, and set them out when danger of frost is past.

When to plant All varieties of squash may be planted whenever soil is warm and easily worked. Dates vary with altitude, area, and likelihood of frost. Consult your local agricultural extension service for best times in your area.

How much To keep a hungry family of five well supplied—including squash for freezing, storage and canning—you should plant 1/8 ounce (1 packet) of summer squash seed (enough for a 25-foot row) and 1/2 ounce (1 packet) of winter squash seed (enough for a 50-foot row). However, most home gardeners will want to scale this down considerably. For example, two or three hills of zucchini will produce enough for a family of four.

Caution To avoid growing strange hybrids, separate squash varieties as much as you can. If planted too close together, acorn and zucchini (for example) have been known to get overly friendly and produce something that looks like a corrugated green banana, and doesn't taste much better.

Weeding As soon as the tiny plants appear, so will the weeds. During this period, crucial to the young plants' growth, weed carefully by hand, avoiding disturbing soil around squash roots. When plants are well-established, thin them (see "How to plant").

Mulch To conserve moisture and prevent weed growth, use a mulch such as straw, old leaves, wood shavings, peat moss, sawdust or black plastic. Wait until plants are established and ground is warm before applying mulch. You will probably find that with black plastic you not only prevent weeds and preserve soil moisture, but also get your squash crop a week or two earlier, since the plastic actually raises the soil

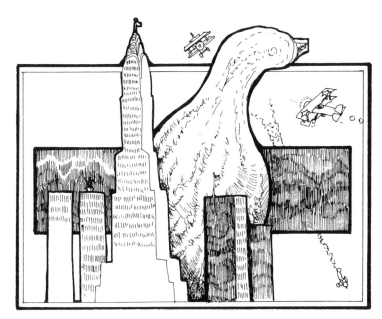

temperature. However, it has the disadvantage of being a nonorganic mulch, so soil is not enriched.

Watering should be frequent but not heavy, to insure steady growth and maximum production. Try to water only around roots, not the foliage.

Cultivation should be shallow, at least 6 inches away from the plant, from the time plants appear until the vines have grown into the rows (when cultivation would injure them). After that, weed regularly, as weeds will take nourishment needed by plants.

Fertilizing Add a good commercial balanced fertilizer before vines begin to run. Rate: Use 1/2 to 1 ounce per hill, applied in a ring 6 inches away from plants and covered with 1 inch of soil. Too much fertilizer, or fertilizer applied too late in the season, will cause plants to run to vine rather than produce fruit, so don't be over generous.

Pests and diseases to watch for, and what to do First, keep your garden tidy and clean, free of weeds and sickly plants. Then, if trouble starts, try natural methods and botanical controls. Only as a last resort, use chemical sprays and powders, and only after carefully reading instructions. Take special note of instructions for using chemicals on food crops.

This is not a complete list of problems and solutions. See gardening encyclopedias and current books on organic gardening for more pointers. The following are among the most prevalent pests and diseases that afflict squash gardens.

Aphids Soft-bodied, tiny insects of various colors: green, black, yellow. Spray with a strong stream of water, soapy water or garlic-water spray.

Corn earworms Light green to brown with alternating light and dark stripes the length of a full-grown, 2-inch body. Handpick worms and destroy.

Cucumber beetles Yellow and black striped when adults. They feast on leaves and stems of young plants. Handpick; protect young plants with screen-wire cages; interplant with radishes.

Curly top This may affect young squash plants, stunting growth and affecting size and number of fruits. Spread by insects; leaves appear curled with irregularly swollen veins. The best solution is to pull up and destroy diseased plants.

Squash bugs Red-brown to black bug, 1/2 to 3/4 inch long. Handpick eggs from underside of leaves; dust plants with mixed wood ashes and hydrated lime.

Squash vine borer Where you see a hole in the vine near base of runner, with yellowish material coming out, slit stalk and stab the grub. Heap a shovelful of soil over the cut stem to protect it and encourage rooting.

If you find that chemicals are the only way to control the above pests and diseases in your garden, some of the most commonly used are rotenone, ryania, and sevin dust. Again, care must be taken if you decide to use these chemical controls; follow the package directions explicitly.

14

When to harvest Summer squash in general take 60 to 75 days from planting date to harvest time, depending on your local conditions. Most winter squash take 100 to 150 days, but acorn and butternut ripen faster (80 to 105 days).

Always cut squash stems with a sharp knife; never break them, or pull squash from the vine.

Look for the same qualities in squash that you harvest from your garden as in those you buy in the market (see page 9).

Gardeners must be especially vigilant for zucchini and other green-skinned squash that are getting too large (12 inches is about the limit). They are difficult to spot among the leaves and grow to maturity rapidly—a matter of 3 to 5 days. Check your vines every day. Besides giving you inferior squash, leaving summer squash on the vine until they reach maturity will cause plants to run to vine rather than produce fruit.

Winter squash are mature when stems turn from dark green to light greenish-yellow, but may be left on the vine another 2 weeks or until stem turns grayish and shrivels. If left in sun 2 weeks after reaching maturity, squash will store better, as much of the water content will have evaporated.

Even before you harvest squash, try picking a few squash blossoms. They are not only decorative as garnishes for salads and cooked dishes—they are good to eat. *Keeping squash* Summer squash will keep up to 1 week in the crisper, in paper or plastic bags. But avoid excessive storage; they are at their best when very fresh.

Winter squash to be stored should be thick-shelled, hard and unblemished. They should be full grown, not frosted or bruised, and with an inch or so of the stem on. Do not store winter squash in more than two layers, to avoid bruising or breaking the skin. Keep in a dry, somewhat dark place, where temperature does not go below 40°F nor approach 70°; ideally, 45° to 55°.

All winter squash will shrink some, but Hubbard the least. Properly stored, they will keep until well after New Year's, sometimes until spring.

appetizers soups & salads

SQUASH IN A DIP

Zucchini combines well with other ingredients for appetizer dips. Shred it and mix it with mayonnaise, sour cream or yoghurt; add chopped pickles, grated cheese, nuts, grated carrots, minced clams, etc. These are good dips for potato chips and also good spreads for crackers, melba toast, flatbread, etc. You may substitute cocozelle, caserta or chayote for the zucchini.

ZUCCHINI DIP I

1 cup finely shredded zucchini
1 cup plain yoghurt

2 garlic cloves, minced
salt to taste

Mix all ingredients, cover and chill. Stir before serving.

ZUCCHINI DIP II

1 cup finely shredded zucchini
3 small green onions, finely chopped
2 tablespoons chopped parsley
2 tablespoons fresh lemon juice

1 garlic clove, minced
salt and pepper to taste
approximately 1/2 cup mayonnaise

Mix all ingredients, adding enough mayonnaise for desired consistency. Cover and chill. Good with not-too-highly-flavored crackers or chips.

ZUCCHINI DIP III

2 cups diced zucchini
2 tablespoons chopped onion
1/2 teaspoon minced garlic
1/2 teaspoon salt
1/8 teaspoon paprika
1/4 teaspoon pepper

1/2 teaspoon dried basil
1 3-ounce package cream cheese,
  at room temperature
1 teaspoon Worcestershire sauce
2 tablespoons fresh lemon juice

Steam zucchini over gently boiling water until soft, about 5 minutes. Cool and combine with onion, garlic and seasonings. Purée in blender until smooth. Add cream cheese and blend. Add remaining ingredients, adjust seasonings and chill. Serve with saltines.

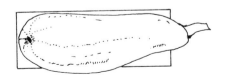

SQUASH WITH A DIP

Summer squash and other raw vegetables (crudités), served with a dip, make good low-calorie cocktail accompaniments or appetizers. Use several varieties of squash: zucchini, crookneck, cymlings, etc. You may add carrots, turnips, celery, jicama, green bell pepper, radishes, cucumbers, in sticks or thin slices; cauliflowerets, green beans, asparagus, and small whole tomatoes and green onions. Serve with any of the preceding dips, or the following.

CRUDITÉ DIP I

1 8-ounce package cream cheese,
   at room temperature
1/2 pound blue cheese, crumbled

2 tablespoons dry vermouth
1 garlic clove, minced
approximately 1 cup sour cream

Combine the cheeses, vermouth and garlic. Add just enough sour cream to make a thinnish dip suitable for dunking the vegetables.

CRUDITÉ DIP II

1 cup mayonnaise
2 teaspoons Dijon-style mustard

1 teaspoon minced garlic

Combine ingredients, mix well, cover and chill. This is also good served over cooked, cooled sliced zucchini.

CYMLING CHIPS WITH TAHINI DIP

Cymling Chips
4 medium cymlings, washed, trimmed
　　and cut in 1/4-inch wedges
1/2 teaspoon salt

Tahini Dip
1/2 cup tahini (sesame seed paste,
　　obtained in Middle Eastern shops)
2/3 cup water
1/4 cup olive oil

6 tablespoons fresh lemon juice
4 garlic cloves, peeled
2 cups cooked, drained garbanzos
　　(chickpeas)
1/2 teaspoon ground cumin
1 teaspoon ground coriander
5 green onions, chopped
1 teaspoon salt
1/2 teaspoon freshly ground pepper

Steam squash for 5 minutes. Drain well, sprinkle with salt and chill. Combine first 5 ingredients for dip in blender and blend until smooth and light-colored. Add garbanzos and spices and blend to a purée. Mix in green onions and salt and pepper. Adjust seasonings and serve in a bowl on a platter surrounded by cymling chips.

ZUCCHINI COLD DISH

1 cup plain yoghurt
1/2 teaspoon salt
1/4 teaspoon pepper
1 teaspoon caraway seeds, crushed

1 medium cucumber, peeled,
　　seeded and grated
2 medium zucchini, grated

Beat yoghurt until smooth and add remaining ingredients. Mix well and chill. Good as antipasto or served with curries.

SQUASH SEED SNACKS

This makes a crunchy, nut-flavored cocktail accompaniment, and is a good way to utilize the nutrition of squash seeds. Use butternut, Delicata or any other winter squash seeds that are not too thick-skinned.

Remove all fiber and pulp clinging to the seeds and spread them on a pie plate or cookie sheet. Dot with butter, sprinkle with salt and place in a 200° oven for about 2 hours, stirring occasionally. Vary flavor by adding garlic powder or curry powder.

ZUCCHINI WITH GARLIC SAUCE

Garlic Sauce
1 cup mayonnaise
1/2 teaspoon dry mustard
2 garlic cloves, minced
2 tablespoons plain yoghurt

3 medium zucchini, cut in strips
2 tablespoons minced chives

Mix ingredients for garlic sauce and chill. Cook zucchini until just tender, about 6 or 7 minutes. Cool, then cover with chilled garlic sauce and sprinkle with chives.
Serves 6

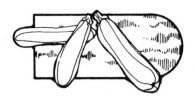

ZUCCHINI-PROSCIUTTO ROLL-UPS

1 5-inch zucchini, washed, trimmed
   and grated

4 very thin slices prosciutto
1 lime, quartered

Blanch grated zucchini in a small amount of water for 1 minute. Drain. Cool. Divide zucchini onto prosciutto slices, roll up and secure with a toothpick. Accompany each serving with a lime wedge.
Serves 4

COOK-AHEAD ZUCCHINI APPETIZER

1-1/2 cups bread crumbs (preferably
   lightly toasted French bread)
1 tablespoon chopped parsley
1 teaspoon salt
1/2 teaspoon dried basil

1/2 teaspoon dried rosemary
1/4 teaspoon dried sage
1/2 teaspoon minced garlic
1/4 cup olive oil
3 or 4 medium zucchini, cut in half
   lengthwise

Whirl all ingredients except zucchini in a blender. Arrange squash cut side up in baking pan and sprinkle with the seasoned bread crumbs. Bake uncovered in a 350° oven 30 minutes, basting occasionally with more olive oil. When cool, cut crosswise into serving-sized pieces.
Serves 6 to 8

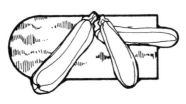

SUMMER SQUASH APPETIZER PLATE

4 medium zucchini
8 small cymlings
1/3 cup olive oil
3 tablespoons wine vinegar
2 tablespoons chopped green bell pepper
1/4 cup chopped green onion
3 tablespoons chopped parsley
1 tablespoon Dijon-style mustard
1 teaspoon salt
1/2 teaspoon pepper
1 2-ounce can anchovy fillets
12 to 16 cherry tomatoes, halved
pitted ripe olives, sliced

Cut off ends of zucchini and scrub well. Trim stems from cymlings and scrub well. Bring a small amount of water to boil and simmer squash about 8 minutes or until just tender. Cool squash. Cut zucchini lengthwise in quarters. Combine next 8 ingredients in a bowl, mix well and adjust seasonings. Add squash and cover for 2 hours. Drain off dressing and reserve. Arrange 4 zucchini strips and 2 whole cymlings on each of 4 salad plates. Garnish with anchovy fillets, tomatoes and olives, and spoon a little reserved dressing over each serving.
Serves 4

SQUASH SPEARS AND PROSCIUTTO

2 4-inch zucchini, washed, trimmed and
  cut in long, thin spears
4 very thin slices prosciutto
4 tablespoons grated Parmesan cheese

Cook zucchini spears in a small amount of water for 5 minutes or until tender. Cool. Divide zucchini onto prosciutto slices, roll up and secure with a toothpick. Place on a buttered cookie sheet and sprinkle with Parmesan cheese. Place in a 400° oven for about 3 minutes or until cheese is melted.
Serves 4

BROTH PICK-ME-UP

2 small zucchini, chopped
2 broccoli stalks, chopped
2 celery stalks, chopped
1 cup cauliflowerets
1 small green bell pepper, chopped

2 12-ounce cans tomato juice
1 tablespoon minced dill
  (or 1 teaspoon dried)
salt and pepper to taste

Combine all ingredients and cook over medium heat about 20 minutes. Put through food mill, adjust seasonings and serve hot or cold.
Serves 6

SUMMER SQUASH-SAUSAGE SOUP

1 pound hot Italian sausage or
  chorizo sausage, sliced
1 cup thinly sliced celery
1 cup chopped onion
2 garlic cloves, minced
2 pounds summer squash (zucchini,
  yellow or cymlings), cut in
  1/2-inch pieces

6 cups chopped peeled tomatoes
  (or 2 28-ounce cans tomatoes
  with juice, chopped)
1 teaspoon dried oregano
1/2 teaspoon dried basil
1-1/2 teaspoons salt
2 garlic cloves, minced
2 cups rich chicken stock
chopped parsley for garnish

Brown sausage in a skillet, drain off fat and add celery, onion and garlic. Cook slowly until onion is translucent, 5 to 10 minutes. Place in a large pot and add remaining ingredients. Bring to a boil, lower heat, cover and simmer 45 minutes to 1 hour. Sprinkle with parsley and serve.
Serves 8

23

WINTER SQUASH SOUP

1 medium onion, chopped
2 tablespoons butter
1/2 teaspoon salt
1/4 teaspoon pepper
2 cups chicken stock

1 cup milk
1/4 teaspoon ground nutmeg
1-1/2 cups puréed cooked winter squash
  (any variety)

Sauté onion in butter until translucent. Add salt and pepper. Remove from heat and gradually stir in stock and milk. Bring to a boil, stirring constantly. Add nutmeg and squash, stirring to blend in, lower heat and cook until heated through. Adjust seasonings.
Serves 6

Variation For a thicker soup, beat 1 egg yolk with 1/2 cup half-and-half. Stir some of the hot soup into the egg mixture, then add to the soup. Heat thoroughly.

MONTEGO BAY BUTTERNUT SQUASH SOUP

3 carrots, peeled and sliced
1/4 pound slab bacon
8 peppercorns
1 garlic clove, sliced
1/2 cup chopped celery with leaves
2 teaspoons chopped parsley
1/2 teaspoon dried thyme
1 bay leaf

1 large potato, peeled and cubed
1 butternut squash (about 2 pounds),
  peeled, seeded and cubed
1 tablespoon sugar
1 teaspoon salt
3 tablespoons dark rum
2 tablespoons fresh lime juice
chopped parsley for garnish

Bring first 8 ingredients to a boil with 2 quarts water, cover and simmer 1 hour. Add potato, squash, sugar and salt and cook 40 minutes or until vegetables are tender. Let cool slightly, remove bacon and bay leaf and pour through sieve or colander. Reserve vegetables. Cool broth and skim off fat. (If possible, let stand several hours or overnight in refrigerator so fat will be easier to remove.)

Put vegetables through food mill or ricer, add to broth and heat. Stir in rum and lime juice and adjust seasonings; simmer 5 minutes. Serve in heated bowls, garnished with chopped parsley.

Serves 8

CHICKEN-ZUCCHINI SOUP

1 large onion, chopped
1 garlic clove, minced
2 tablespoons peanut or corn oil
2 large zucchini, sliced
1-1/2 cups chopped peeled tomatoes

1/2 teaspoon dried thyme
2 cups tomato juice
2 cups chicken stock or water
salt and pepper to taste
2 cups diced cooked chicken

Sauté onion and garlic in a saucepan in oil until golden. Add remaining ingredients, except chicken, and simmer covered for 20 minutes or until flavors are blended. Add chicken and simmer 5 minutes. Adjust seasonings and serve.
Serves 6

COLD SQUASH BISQUE

4 cups chicken stock
3 cups sliced zucchini or cocozelle
1/2 cup chopped onion
1/4 cup rice
1 tablespoon curry powder
1/2 tablespoon dry mustard

1 teaspoon salt
1/2 teaspoon pepper
1-1/2 cups cold milk
plain yoghurt or sour cream
thinly sliced green onions or
    chopped chives for garnish

Simmer together all ingredients except milk, yoghurt and garnishes until squash and rice are tender. Put through food mill and chill 6 hours or overnight. Just before serving stir in milk. Top each bowl with a dollop of yoghurt or sour cream. Garnish with onions or chives.
Serves 6

CREAM OF ZUCCHINI SOUP

1 large zucchini, thinly sliced
1/2 onion, chopped
2 cups chicken stock
1/2 cup heavy cream

1/2 teaspoon dried tarragon
salt and pepper to taste
chopped parsley for garnish

Cook zucchini and onion in chicken stock until tender. Put through food mill and return to saucepan. Bring to a simmer and stir in cream. Season with tarragon, salt and pepper and heat through. Serve immediately, garnished with parsley. This soup can also be served cold.
Serves 4

CHAYOTE SOUP

3 medium chayotes, peeled and cubed
1 cup chopped onion
1 garlic clove, minced
2 tablespoons butter
1 tablespoon flour
4 cups chicken stock, heated

1 cup shredded cooked chicken
1 teaspoon salt
1/4 teaspoon white pepper
chopped coriander for garnish
paper-thin lime slices for garnish

Cook squash in 2 cups boiling salted water until tender, about 20 minutes. Purée in blender with the cooking water; set aside. Sauté onion and garlic in butter until golden. Stir in flour. When smooth, add chicken stock slowly, stirring until smooth. Add puréed squash and cook 5 minutes, stirring occasionally. Add chicken and cook until heated through. Add salt and pepper and adjust seasonings. Garnish with coriander and lime slices.
Serves 6

COLD SQUASH SALAD

6 medium summer squash (yellow,
cymling or zucchini), sliced
1/4 inch thick
1/2 teaspoon salt
1 tablespoon chopped parsley
6 peppercorns
dried thyme to taste
1 bay leaf

1 tablespoon fresh lime juice
1 tablespoon fresh lemon juice
1 garlic clove, crushed
lettuce leaves
freshly ground pepper
2 tablespoons grated Parmesan cheese
olive oil

Bring 1 cup water to boil in a kettle and add all ingredients except lettuce, pepper, cheese and oil. Lower heat and simmer until squash is just tender. Drain, remove bay leaf and garlic clove and chill squash. Place squash on lettuce leaves, grind pepper over and sprinkle with Parmesan cheese. Drizzle lightly with olive oil.
Serves 4 to 6

ZUCCHINI-APPLE SALAD

1/3 cup safflower oil
1 tablespoon fresh lemon juice
2 tablespoons white wine vinegar
1 teaspoon dried basil
1 teaspoon salt

2 or 3 red apples, cored and diced
1/2 white onion, thinly sliced
1 pound zucchini, thinly sliced
1 green bell pepper, cut in
long thin strips

Mix oil, lemon juice, vinegar, basil and salt in a large salad bowl. Add apples, coating well. Add onion slices, zucchini slices and green pepper strips. Mix gently, then chill.
Serves 6

GREEK SALAD WITH CYMLINGS

1 small head romaine lettuce
1 small head Boston lettuce
6 medium cymlings, 3 to 4 inches in
    diameter, trimmed, washed and
    cut in eighths
salt
1 green bell pepper, trimmed, seeded
    and cut in 1/4-inch strips
4 green onions, chopped

1/4 pound kasseri cheese, cut in
    1/2-inch cubes
3/8 cup olive oil
2 tablespoons red wine vinegar
1/2 teaspoon salt
1/4 teaspoon freshly ground pepper
12 cherry tomatoes, washed and
    stems removed
12 Greek olives

Wash lettuces, dry thoroughly, tear in bite-size pieces and chill. Steam squash for 10 minutes, or cook in small amount of water for 5 minutes. Drain, sprinkle with salt and chill. Combine lettuce, squash, green pepper, onions and cheese in a large bowl. Combine oil, vinegar, salt and pepper and toss with salad. Garnish with tomatoes and olives.

Serves 6 to 8

AVOCADO-ZUCCHINI SALAD

1 lemon
1 ripe avocado, peeled and sliced
   in crescents
4 cups shredded zucchini
cherry tomatoes, halved

1 head Boston or leaf lettuce,
   torn into pieces
1/3 cup sour cream
2 teaspoons dry mustard
freshly ground pepper to taste
1/4 teaspoon Worcestershire sauce

Squeeze lemon juice onto avocado slices; chill. Mix zucchini and tomatoes in salad bowl with lettuce. In a small bowl mix sour cream, mustard, pepper and Worcestershire sauce and pour over salad. Place avocado slices on top.
Serves 4

ZUCCHINI-RICE SALAD

3 medium zucchini, thinly sliced
2 cups cooled cooked rice
1/2 cup thinly sliced green onions
1/2 cup chopped parsley
3 tablespoons olive oil
1/3 cup white wine vinegar

1/2 teaspoon finely minced garlic
1 teaspoon minced thyme
salt, pepper and cayenne pepper to taste
lettuce leaves
parsley sprigs

Combine zucchini, rice, onions and parsley in a large salad bowl. In a small bowl, mix oil, vinegar, garlic, thyme, salt, pepper and cayenne. Pour over zucchini-rice mixture, stir and chill. Serve on lettuce leaves and garnish with parsley sprigs.
Serves 6

ITALIAN SALAD BOWL

2 cups sliced zucchini
1/2 cup sliced radishes
3 green onions, sliced
1 cup sliced mushrooms
romaine, butter or leaf lettuce,
    torn in small pieces

1/4 cup olive oil
2 tablespoons white wine vinegar
salt and freshly ground pepper to taste
1/2 cup crumbled blue cheese

Combine vegetables and mushrooms in a salad bowl with the salad greens. Mix oil and vinegar and pour over salad. Add salt and pepper to taste and sprinkle crumbled blue cheese over top.
Serves 6

TUNA-ZUCCHINI SALAD

1 7-ounce can tuna
2 medium zucchini, shredded
2 small carrots, shredded
1/3 cup mayonnaise
1 teaspoon Dijon-style mustard

1/4 teaspoon celery salt
lettuce leaves
freshly ground pepper
tomato slices (optional)
thinly sliced Bermuda onion (optional)

Drain tuna, flake it and place in a bowl with zucchini and carrots. In another bowl, combine mayonnaise, mustard and celery salt. Add dressing to tuna-zucchini mixture and mix lightly. Serve on individual salad plates with lettuce leaves. Grind pepper over and surround with tomato slices and onion slices.
Serves 4

31

HOT POTATO SALAD

4 medium potatoes
2 small yellow straightneck, crook-
    neck or zucchini, sliced 1/8 inch
    thick
2 tablespoons olive oil
1/4 cup chopped onion
1/4 cup chopped celery
1 garlic clove, minced

1/4 pound mortadella, cut in
    1/2-inch cubes
1/4 cup water
1/2 cup red wine vinegar
1/2 teaspoon sugar
1 teaspoon salt
1/8 teaspoon paprika
1/4 teaspoon dry mustard

Cook potatoes in their jackets in a covered saucepan until tender. Peel and slice them while hot and keep them warm. Steam squash 10 minutes; drain, keep warm. Heat olive oil in a skillet and sauté onion, celery, garlic and mortadella until onion is golden, stirring frequently. Combine remaining ingredients in a saucepan and bring to boiling point. Pour into skillet, then combine the hot dressing with hot potatoes and squash, mixing gently.

Serves 4 to 6

HOT YELLOW SQUASH SALAD

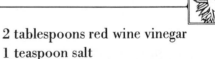

6 small yellow crookneck or
    straightneck, thinly sliced
1/2 cup olive oil

2 tablespoons red wine vinegar
1 teaspoon salt
freshly ground pepper to taste

Sauté squash in half of the oil for 1 minute; cover, lower heat and cook 4 minutes longer. Mix remaining oil with red wine vinegar and add salt and pepper. Pour over squash slices and mix until slices are coated. Serve at once.

Serves 6

squash as accompaniment

SUMMER SQUASH PURÉE

1-1/2 pounds summer squash (any
    variety), thinly sliced
1-1/2 tablespoons butter

1/2 teaspoon salt
1/4 teaspoon pepper

Cook squash in small amount of boiling water until tender, about 6 minutes. Put squash through food mill or potato ricer. Add butter, salt, and pepper.
Serves 3 to 4

Variation Combine puréed squash with 2 beaten eggs in a buttered shallow casserole. Sprinkle with 1/2 cup grated Parmesan cheese, set dish in a larger one filled with hot water to 1/2 inch and bake at 350° for 30 minutes.

33

CYMLING SQUASH BAKE

4 cymlings
1 small onion, grated

3/4 cup grated Cheddar or Gruyère
   cheese

Trim, split cymlings in half horizontally and drop into a small amount of boiling water. Cook until almost tender, about 5 minutes; drain. Place in a shallow buttered baking dish, cut side up. Sprinkle cheese and grated onion on top of each cymling half. Bake in a 350° oven for 10 to 15 minutes or until tender.
Serves 4

STUFFED CYMLINGS (PATTYPANS)

4 medium cymlings
3 tablespoons butter
3 green onions, minced
2 teaspoons ground walnuts

1/3 cup chicken stock
2 tablespoons heavy cream
salt and white pepper to taste
1/2 cup grated Romano cheese

Trim ends and cook squash in boiling water for 5 minutes. Cut a 1/2-inch slice off blossom end of each squash and scoop out pulp, leaving a 1/4-inch shell. Chop pulp and slices finely. In a saucepan melt 2 tablespoons of the butter, add onions and nuts and cook until well blended. Stir in stock and cream slowly and cook until thickened. Add chopped squash, salt and pepper. Fill each cymling with mixture, sprinkle each with Romano cheese and dot with the remaining tablespoon of butter. Bake uncovered in a buttered baking dish in a 350° oven for 25 minutes.
Serves 4

SOUR CREAMED SUMMER SQUASH

1 pound summer squash (any variety), sliced
1 tablespoon melted butter

1/2 teaspoon salt
1/4 teaspoon paprika
1/2 cup sour cream

Combine all ingredients except sour cream. Bake in a buttered casserole in a 350° oven for 40 minutes. Remove from oven, allow to cool slightly and mix in sour cream.
Serves 4

BACON SUMMER SQUASH

4 slices bacon, cut in 1-inch pieces
6 small summer squash (zucchini or crookneck), sliced 1/4 inch thick
1 medium onion, sliced
1/4 cup chopped parsley

1-1/2 cups peeled and chopped tomatoes
1/2 teaspoon salt
1/4 teaspoon pepper
1/2 cup grated mozzarella cheese

In a skillet sauté bacon until brown; pour off drippings. Add squash, onion, parsley, tomatoes, salt and pepper. Cover and steam for 10 to 15 minutes or until tender. Sprinkle cheese on top and cover just until cheese melts.
Serves 4 to 6

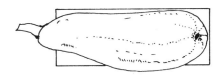

YELLOW AND GREEN SQUASH CASSEROLE

2 medium zucchini, coarsely shredded
2 yellow crookneck or straightneck,
   coarsely shredded
1 onion, chopped
2 tablespoons chopped parsley

3 eggs, beaten
1/2 cup milk
1 cup shredded fontina or Swiss cheese
salt, pepper and dried oregano to taste
1 tablespoon butter

Combine all ingredients except butter, and reserving 1/4 cup of the cheese. Place in a buttered shallow casserole. Sprinkle reserved cheese on top and dot with butter. Bake in a 325° oven for 45 minutes.
Serves 4

COURGETTES À LA NIÇOISE

6 medium zucchini
1/2 cup chopped onion
1/2 cup cooked rice
1 garlic clove, minced
1/4 teaspoon dried tarragon

3 tablespoons tomato paste
3 tablespoons chopped parsley
8 large black olives, chopped
salt and pepper to taste

Trim ends from zucchini and drop zucchini into boiling water for 10 minutes until almost tender. Slice in half lengthwise and scoop out pulp, leaving a 1/2-inch thick shell. Combine pulp with onion, rice, garlic, tarragon, tomato paste, parsley, olives and salt and pepper. Fill shells with mixture and place in a shallow buttered baking dish and bake in a 350° oven for 30 minutes.
Serves 6

SQUASH FRITTERS

2 cups grated summer squash
   (yellow, caserta or zucchini)
1/2 teaspoon minced garlic
1/2 teaspoon salt
1/4 teaspoon pepper

2 tablespoons grated Romano or
   Parmesan cheese
2 eggs, beaten
1 cup all-purpose flour
1 cup corn oil

Mix together all ingredients except oil. Heat oil in a heavy skillet and drop squash mixture into the oil by tablespoonfuls. Cook slowly on medium heat, turning often. Drain fritters on paper toweling.

Serves 4 to 6

Variation Add 1/4 teaspoon dried oregano and 2 tablespoons chopped parsley.

ZUCCHINI FRITTATA

1 onion, chopped
1 garlic clove, minced
6 medium zucchini, sliced
1 tomato, peeled and chopped
2 tablespoons chopped fresh green
   chili pepper (optional)

salt and pepper to taste
dash of dried thyme, basil and oregano
2 tablespoons corn or peanut oil
3 eggs, beaten

In a skillet sauté the onion, garlic, zucchini, tomato and seasonings in the oil. Cook until tender. Pour beaten eggs over, stir gently, cover and cook over low heat until eggs are set. Prick puffed middle with fork. When frittata is set and browned on bottom, slide out and invert onto a platter. Cut in pie-shaped wedges to serve.

Serves 6

ZUCCHINI AND SOUR CREAM

4 to 5 small zucchini, shredded
1 tablespoon peanut oil or corn oil
3 tablespoons hulled sunflower seeds
1/4 teaspoon white pepper

1/2 teaspoon salt
1/2 cup sour cream
2 tablespoons chopped coriander

In a large skillet sauté zucchini in oil for 2 minutes. Add sunflower seeds, white pepper and salt. Cover and simmer until zucchini is just tender. Remove from heat and stir in sour cream and coriander.
Serves 4

SKILLET ZUCCHINI

6 small zucchini, thinly sliced
2 eggs, beaten
1/4 cup flour

1/2 teaspoon salt
1/4 teaspoon pepper
1/4 cup olive oil

Dip zucchini slices in egg, then in flour which has been seasoned with salt and pepper. Sauté in oil in a skillet for 4 to 5 minutes or until tender.
Serves 6

WALNUT ZUCCHINI

4 or 5 medium zucchini,
   sliced 1/2 inch thick
1/2 cup sliced green onions
1/4 cup corn or peanut oil

1/4 cup dry red wine
2 to 3 tablespoons fresh lemon juice
1 cup coarsely chopped walnuts

In a skillet sauté zucchini and onions in oil for 4 to 5 minutes, until zucchini is tender but still crunchy. Add wine and lemon juice and simmer for 5 minutes. Mix in walnuts and serve.

Serves 6

ZUCCHINI WITH CREAM

2 tablespoons chopped green onions
   or shallots
2 tablespoons butter
5 or 6 small zucchini, shredded

1/2 teaspoon salt
1/4 teaspoon pepper
1 tablespoon Dijon-style mustard
1 cup heavy cream

In a skillet sauté green onions or shallots in butter. Add zucchini and salt and pepper and stir and cook for 5 to 6 minutes or until tender. Mix mustard and cream together and pour over zucchini. Simmer over low heat until cream is absorbed by the zucchini.

Serves 4 to 6

ZUCCHINI-CHEESE SHELLS

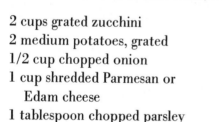

6 zucchini
2 eggs, beaten
1/2 cup small-curd cottage cheese
1/4 cup finely chopped green onions

3/4 cup grated Monterey jack cheese
1/4 cup chopped parsley
salt and pepper to taste

Trim ends from zucchini and drop zucchini into boiling water for 10 minutes until almost tender. Cut in half lengthwise. Scoop out pulp, leaving a 1/4-inch thick shell, and mix pulp with remaining ingredients, reserving about 3 tablespoons of the cheese. Fill shells with mixture and sprinkle reserved cheese on top. Place in a shallow buttered baking dish and bake in a 350° oven for 20 minutes or until tender.
Serves 6

POTATO-ZUCCCHINI PATTIES

2 cups grated zucchini
2 medium potatoes, grated
1/2 cup chopped onion
1 cup shredded Parmesan or
    Edam cheese
1 tablespoon chopped parsley

salt and pepper to taste
2 eggs, beaten
flour
2 tablespoons butter
1 tablespoon corn oil

In a mixing bowl combine zucchini, potatoes, onion, cheese, parsley, salt, pepper and eggs. Mix well and form into 3-inch patties and dust with flour. Heat butter and oil in a skillet until butter foams and fry patties on both sides until golden brown. Drain on paper toweling.
Serves 4 to 6

TWO-CHEESE ZUCCHINI

1 garlic clove, minced
2 tablespoons chopped parsley
4 tablespoons butter, melted
salt and pepper to taste
8 small zucchini, cut in thin strips

1/4 pound feta cheese, cut in
    long thin slices
1/4 pound prosciutto, chopped
2 tablespoons grated Parmesan cheese

Mix together garlic, parsley and melted butter. Add seasonings. Coat each zucchini strip with the mixture and place on a buttered baking sheet. Place a piece of feta cheese on each zucchini strip and sprinkle with prosciutto and grated Parmesan cheese. Broil 4 to 6 minutes until zucchini is tender.
Serves 4

OLIVE-TOMATO ZUCCHINI

1 large onion, sliced
1 garlic clove, minced
3 tablespoons butter
2 tablespoons flour
1 teaspoon salt
1/4 teaspoon pepper

1 teaspoon paprika
2 cups chopped peeled tomatoes
4 medium zucchini, quartered length-
    wise and cut in 2-inch lengths
1 cup pimiento-stuffed green olives,
    sliced

In a skillet sauté onion and garlic in butter until just heated. Stir in flour and seasonings. Add tomatoes and cook and stir until thickened. Add zucchini and simmer, covered, about 10 minutes. Stir in olives and heat through.
Serves 6

STUFFED SQUASH BLOSSOMS

12 squash blossoms

Forcemeat
3/4 cup raw or cooked ground meat
   (chicken, veal or beef)
1 egg white

2 tablespoons grated onion
1/2 teaspoon salt
1/4 teaspoon pepper
1/4 teaspoon dried thyme
1/4 teaspoon dried basil
about 2 tablespoons heavy cream

Combine ingredients for forcemeat, adding just enough cream to hold the mixture together. Gently open petals and place forcemeat in blossoms, using only enough so that the petals will close. Place blossoms in buttered shallow baking dish and heat in a 350° oven for 15 to 20 minutes.
Serves 4

DEEP-FRIED SQUASH BLOSSOMS

1 cup sifted all-purpose flour
1 teaspoon baking powder
1/4 teaspoon salt
1/2 cup milk

2 eggs, beaten
12 large squash blossoms
peanut oil for deep-frying

Combine flour, baking powder and salt. Beat milk and eggs together; stir quickly into dry ingredients. Dip squash blossoms in batter and deep-fry in peanut oil for about 3 minutes. Drain and serve immediately.
Serves 3 or 4

HUBBARD SQUASH AND SOUR CREAM

1 medium onion, sliced
1 tablespoon corn oil
4 cups cooked, diced Hubbard squash
3/4 cup chopped fresh pineapple
  (optional)

1 to 2 teaspoons brown sugar
salt and pepper to taste
1 teaspoon fresh lemon juice
1/2 cup sour cream

In a large skillet sauté onion in oil until translucent. Add squash and pineapple and cook just until heated through. Add brown sugar, seasonings and lemon juice. Simmer 5 minutes. Remove from heat and stir in sour cream.
Serves 4 to 6

BAKED HUBBARD SQUASH

1 3- to 4-pound Hubbard squash
1 tablespoon butter
1 tablespoon honey

1/4 teaspoon salt
milk or cream
finely chopped pecans

Bake squash in a 375° oven for 1 hour or until it is easily pierced with a toothpick. Cut in half, remove seeds and peel. Mash pulp and add butter, honey, salt and enough milk or cream to make a smooth consistency. Sprinkle with nuts and serve immediately.
Serves 4

Variations In place of milk or cream add fresh orange juice, crushed pineapple or lemon juice.

44

HUBBARD SQUASH PATTIES

1 medium potato, cooked,
   peeled and mashed
3 cups mashed cooked Hubbard squash
dried summer savory or sage and salt
   to taste

1 egg, beaten
ground almonds
2 tablespoons butter
1 tablespoon corn oil

Mix potato and squash. Add seasonings and beaten egg. Shape into 3-inch patties and lightly dust with ground almonds. Heat butter and oil in a skillet until butter foams and fry patties on both sides until golden brown. Drain on paper toweling.
Serves 6 to 8

HUBBARD SQUASH SAVORY PUDDING

2 eggs, beaten
1/2 cup milk
2 cups mashed cooked Hubbard squash
1/2 teaspoon salt

1/4 teaspoon pepper
1 tablespoon butter
chopped dill or chives

Combine eggs, milk, squash and salt and pepper. Place in a buttered 1-quart casserole and dot with butter. Set casserole in a pan with hot water to 1 inch and bake in a 350° oven for 30 minutes or until set. Sprinkle with dill or chives.
Serves 4

2 acorn squash, halved lengthwise
with seeds and fibers removed
2 tablespoons butter, at room
temperature

salt
2 teaspoons brown sugar

Rub squash with 2 teaspoons of the butter and place cut side down in a baking dish with hot water to 1/4 inch. Bake 45 minutes in a 350° oven or until tender. Turn cut side up, season lightly with salt and add 1/2 teaspoon brown sugar and 1 teaspoon butter to each half.
Serves 4

Variations
- Add 1 teaspoon chutney to each half
- Add apple slices which have been sautéed in butter to each half
- Use maple syrup in place of brown sugar
- Add 1 tablespoon sherry to each half

ORANGE ACORN SQUASH

3 tablespoons butter, at room
   temperature
3 acorn squash, halved lengthwise
   with seeds and fibers removed

salt to taste
2 oranges, peeled and sectioned
2 tablespoons brown sugar
1/4 cup slivered toasted almonds
2 tablespoons butter

Butter inside of cut squash and sprinkle lightly with salt. Place orange sections in each half, sprinkle with brown sugar and almonds and dot with butter. Bake in a 375° oven 1 hour and 15 minutes in a shallow baking dish with hot water to 1/4 inch. Add additional water if needed during cooking time.
Serves 6

ACORN SQUASH WITH PEAR

2 medium acorn squash, halved lengthwise
   with seeds and fibers removed
1 onion, chopped
2 tablespoons butter
2 fresh pears, peeled, cored and chopped

1/4 teaspoon salt
1/2 teaspoon ground cinnamon
1 tablespoon honey
1 tablespoon sherry

Place squash, cut side down, in a shallow baking dish with hot water to 1/2 inch. Bake in a 400° oven for 20 minutes. While squash is cooking, sauté onion in butter until golden. Stir in chopped pear, salt, cinnamon, honey and sherry. After initial baking period turn squash halves over and mound pear mixture in the centers. Bake 20 to 30 minutes longer in a 375° oven.
Serves 4

SPAGHETTI SQUASH WITH PESTO

1 3-pound spaghetti squash
2 cups chopped fresh basil, or
2 cups chopped fresh parsley with
   2 tablespoons dried basil
1 teaspoon salt
1/2 teaspoon freshly ground pepper

1 teaspoon minced garlic
2 tablespoons finely chopped
   walnuts or pine nuts
1 to 1-1/2 cups olive oil
1/2 cup grated Romano or Parmesan
   cheese

Prepare spaghetti squash as directed in Spaghetti Squash Parmesan, following. Just before squash is done combine all remaining ingredients, except cheese, in a blender, using 1 cup of the olive oil. Blend at high speed until smooth. The sauce should be thin; if necessary blend in up to 1/2 cup more olive oil. Pour into bowl and stir in the grated cheese. Serve over hot spaghetti squash.
Serves 6 to 8

SPAGHETTI SQUASH PARMESAN

1 3-pound spaghetti squash
1/4 pound butter, melted
1/2 cup grated Parmesan cheese
2 tablespoons chopped parsley

1/2 teaspoon salt
1/2 teaspoon freshly ground
   pepper
1/2 teaspoon dried thyme

Pierce the squash in 2 or 3 places with a sharp fork. Place the squash on a cookie sheet and bake in a 350° oven for 1 hour. Turn squash over and bake 45 minutes more or until tender. Slice off stem end and split squash in half lengthwise with a sharp knife. Scoop out seeds and fiber and discard. Loosen flesh with a fork; it will separate into spaghetti-like strands.

Combine remaining ingredients. Place squash on a hot platter and pour cheese sauce over.

Serves 6 to 8

WINTER SQUASH WITH BACON

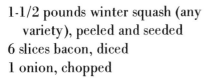

1-1/2 pounds winter squash (any variety), peeled and seeded
6 slices bacon, diced
1 onion, chopped

1 garlic clove, minced
1/4 cup water
1 tablespoon fresh lemon juice

Cut squash into small cubes. You should have about 4 cups. Fry bacon until crisp; drain, reserving 3 tablespoons of the drippings, and set bacon aside. Sauté onion and garlic in drippings until onion is translucent. Add squash and water and cook over medium heat for 15 minutes, covered. Add reserved bacon and lemon juice and serve.

Serves 4

QUICK SQUASH CUSTARD FOR TWO

1/2 cup mashed cooked winter squash
   (any variety)
1/4 cup milk
2 tablespoons sugar
1 egg

1/4 teaspoon ground nutmeg
1/2 teaspoon salt
1/4 cup ground filberts or other nuts
   (optional)

Whirl all ingredients in blender for 1 minute. Pour into 2 custard cups, place cups in a pan with hot water to 1/2 inch and bake in a 375° oven for 30 minutes or until a knife comes out clean. Serve while warm, or chill until served.
Serves 2

WINTER SQUASH PURÉE

3 pounds winter squash (any variety),
   cut in pieces with seeds removed
3 tablespoons butter

1 teaspoon salt
1/2 teaspoon pepper
1/4 teaspoon ground nutmeg

Cook squash in boiling water to cover until tender. Cool. Peel off skin. Put squash through a food mill or potato ricer. Add butter, salt, pepper and nutmeg.
Serves 6

meatless main dishes

TRICOLOR SQUASH DISH

2 cups peeled, cubed banana squash
12 pearl onions, halved
3 tablespoons butter
2 cups cubed zucchini
1 cup cubed cymlings
1/4 cup chopped parsley

1 teaspoon salt
1/2 teaspoon dried thyme
1/2 teaspoon dried basil
1/2 cup sour cream
chopped chives for garnish

Cook banana squash in a small amount of salted water until just tender. Drain and set aside. Sauté onions in butter until translucent. Add zucchini, cymlings and seasonings; cover and cook gently until just tender, stirring occasionally to prevent burning. Combine with banana squash in a buttered casserole and place in a 350° oven for 5 or 10 minutes to heat thoroughly. Add sour cream and mix gently. Garnish with chives.
Serves 4

Squash Ring
3 cups mashed cooked winter squash
3 tablespoons butter, melted
1 tablespoon grated onion
3 eggs, beaten
1/2 teaspoon ground nutmeg
1 teaspoon salt

Creamed Peas Filling
2 cups freshly shelled peas
  (2 pounds unshelled)
2 tablespoons butter
2 tablespoons flour
1 cup milk
1/4 teaspoon salt
ground nutmeg for garnish

Combine all ingredients for squash ring, place in a buttered ring mold and bake in a 350° oven for 1 hour or until brown. Just before squash ring is done, cook peas in a small amount of simmering salted water for 5 minutes or until tender. Drain and set aside. Melt butter over low heat, add flour and blend over low heat for 3 to 5 minutes. Stir in milk slowly, stirring constantly to avoid lumps. Cook, stirring with wire whisk or wooden spoon until thick and smooth. Combine with peas. Turn squash out of mold onto a heated platter. Pour creamed peas into center of squash ring and sprinkle nutmeg over top.
Serves 4 to 6

Variations Fill ring with other vegetables, creamed or simply seasoned with salt, pepper and butter, such as green beans, cauliflower, broccoli or Brussels sprouts; or creamed mushrooms, chicken or turkey.

2 small zucchini or other summer
  squash
1 medium eggplant (1 to 1-1/4 pounds)
4 cups water
1 tablespoon salt
6 small dried black mushrooms
2 green bell peppers
3 tablespoons Szechwan chili paste
  (chili paste with garlic,
  available in Chinese shops)

1 tablespoon soy sauce
2 tablespoons dry sherry
1-1/2 tablespoons red wine vinegar
1 teaspoon sugar
1 teaspoon salt
5/8 cup peanut oil
1/2 cup water

As with any stir-fry dish, have all ingredients ready before you begin. Trim ends of squash and eggplant; cut in 1-inch cubes. Place in a bowl with water and salt for 5 to 10 minutes. Drain well. Soak mushrooms in hot water to cover for 15 to 30 minutes; drain, squeeze to extract most of the moisture, cut off and discard tough stems. Remove stems and seeds from pepper and cut in 1-inch squares. Blend together chili paste, soy sauce, sherry, vinegar, sugar and salt. Heat 1/2 cup oil in wok or skillet; add eggplant and squash, stirring and pressing, and cook until lightly browned, about 5 minutes. Remove and drain. Add remaining 2 tablespoons oil to wok, heat oil, and stir-fry mushrooms and peppers for about 1 to 2 minutes. Return eggplant and squash and stir-fry 5 minutes. Add water and cook, stirring, 5 seconds. Add soy sauce mixture and cook, stirring, 1 minute. Serve at once.
Serves 6

STUFFED ZUCCHINI

6 small zucchini
1 cup minced mushrooms
1 egg, beaten
1/2 cup grated Parmesan cheese

2 tablespoons chopped basil
  (or 2 teaspoons dried)
salt and pepper to taste
1 tablespoon butter

Trim ends from zucchini and drop zucchini into boiling water for 8 minutes until lightly cooked. Slice zucchini in half lengthwise and scoop out pulp, leaving a 1/4-inch thick shell. Combine pulp with mushrooms, egg, all but 2 tablespoons of the cheese and seasonings. Place mixture in zucchini shells, sprinkle with remaining cheese and dot with butter. Place in a shallow buttered baking dish and bake in a 325° oven for 30 minutes.
Serves 4

EGGPLANT-ZUCCHINI CASSEROLE

1 medium eggplant, cut in
  1/2-inch thick slices
salt
2 medium zucchini, thinly sliced
2 onions, sliced
2 tomatoes, peeled and thinly sliced

1/2 cup olive oil
salt and pepper to taste
1/2 teaspoon dried basil
1/2 teaspoon dried thyme
2 tablespoons chopped parsley
3/4 cup crumbled feta cheese

Lightly salt eggplant slices and let stand 15 minutes. In a greased 1-1/2-quart casserole alternate layers of eggplant, zucchini, onions and tomatoes, dribbling olive oil and sprinkling seasonings on each layer. Sprinkle cheese on top and lightly dribble with olive oil. Bake in a 350° oven for 45 minutes.
Serves 6

1 onion, chopped
2 garlic cloves, minced
1/4 cup olive oil
6 small summer squash (cymlings, yellow or zucchini), thinly sliced
1/2 pound green beans, cut in 2-inch pieces
2 carrots, sliced
1/2 pound green peas, shelled
2 potatoes, peeled and cut in long thin strips

2 celery stalks, cut in 1-inch pieces
1 medium chayote, sliced 3/4 inch thick
2 ripe tomatoes, peeled and chopped
3/4 cup vegetable or chicken stock
1/2 teaspoon dried thyme or sweet marjoram
salt and pepper to taste
chopped parsley for garnish

Sauté onion and garlic in oil until onion is translucent. Combine onion and garlic with remaining ingredients and place in a buttered 2-quart casserole. Bake, covered, in a 325° oven for 1 hour or until vegetables are tender. Garnish with parsley.
Serves 6 to 8

SKILLET SUMMER SQUASH

1 medium onion, chopped
1 green bell pepper, chopped
3 pounds summer squash (any variety), diced
3 tablespoons corn or peanut oil
2 large tomatoes, peeled and diced
1/2 pound mushrooms, chopped

2 tablespoons chopped parsley
1/4 teaspoon ground turmeric
salt and white pepper to taste
3/4 cup freshly grated corn kernels
1 teaspoon brown sugar
1/2 cup plain yoghurt
1 tablespoon fresh lemon juice

In a skillet sauté onion, green pepper and squash in hot oil for about 3 minutes. Add tomatoes, mushrooms, parsley and seasonings. Simmer covered for 10 minutes. Add corn and simmer for another 5 minutes. Remove from heat and stir in sugar, yoghurt and lemon juice.

Serves 6

ZUCCHINI-STUFFED TOMATOES

6 large tomatoes
2 or 3 small zucchini, grated
1/2 cup chopped watercress
1 cup grated Swiss cheese

1 cup cooked brown rice
2 green onions, minced
salt and pepper to taste
watercress sprigs for garnish

Cut off tops of tomatoes and scoop out pulp to make a shell 1/4 inch thick, reserving pulp. Turn shells upside down and let drain for 10 minutes. Combine pulp, grated zucchini, watercress, cheese, rice, onions and salt and pepper. Fill tomato shells with mixture. Bake in a shallow buttered baking dish in a 325° oven for 25 minutes. Garnish with watercress sprigs.

Serves 6

SQUASH OVEN OMELET

6 medium summer squash (yellow, zucchini, cymlings or combination), chopped
2 tablespoons minced onion
1 garlic clove, minced
3 tablespoons olive oil

2 tablespoons butter
2 tablespoons dry white wine
2 tablespoons chopped parsley
4 eggs, well beaten
1/2 cup grated Parmesan or Romano cheese

Sauté squash, onion and garlic in olive oil and butter in a skillet until almost tender. Mix in wine, parsley, eggs and cheese and pour into a 1-1/2 quart buttered casserole. Bake in a 325° oven for 30 minutes.

Serves 6

ZUCCHINI AND SPINACH NOODLES

1 onion, chopped
1 garlic clove, minced
3 tablespoons olive oil
1/4 cup minced parsley
1-1/2 cups chopped, peeled tomatoes
1/2 cup dry red wine

1/4 teaspoon each salt and pepper
1 2-ounce jar chopped pimientos,
  drained
3 medium zucchini, thinly sliced
12 ounces spinach noodles
grated Parmesan cheese

Cook onion and garlic in oil until onion is translucent. Add parsley, tomatoes, wine and salt and pepper. Bring to a boil, stirring occasionally. Reduce heat, cover and simmer for 30 minutes. Stir in pimientos and zucchini and cook covered, about 5 minutes or until zucchini is tender.

Cook the noodles in boiling salted water until just tender. Drain, place in a serving dish and pour sauce over noodles. Serve Parmesan on the side.
Serves 4

SUMMER SQUASH SOUFFLÉ

1 pound summer squash (zucchini,
  cymlings, yellow), cooked
  and mashed
1/4 cup grated Swiss cheese
1 tablespoon heavy cream

1 tablespoon butter, melted
1/2 teaspoon salt
1/4 teaspoon white pepper
1/4 teaspoon dried thyme
2 eggs, separated

Combine squash, cheese, cream, butter and seasonings. Lightly beat egg yolks and add to squash mixture. Beat egg whites until stiff and fold into mixture. Place in a buttered 1-1/2-quart casserole and bake in a 375° oven for 20 to 30 minutes.
Serves 4
58

1 cup hot cooked and puréed
    winter squash
2 tablespoons butter
1/2 teaspoon salt
1/4 teaspoon white pepper
2 eggs, separated

Cheese Sauce
1 tablespoon butter
1 tablespoon flour
3/4 cup milk
1/2 cup grated Cheddar cheese
1/2 teaspoon salt
1/8 teaspoon paprika
1/4 teaspoon dry mustard

Mix together squash, butter, salt, pepper and egg yolks; cool. Beat egg whites until stiff; fold gently into squash mixture. Pour into 2 individual custard cups or soufflé dishes and bake in a 350° oven for 50 minutes.

While soufflés are cooking, melt butter for cheese sauce, stir in flour and blend. Stir milk in slowly and cook and stir until smooth and thickened. Reduce heat and stir in cheese and seasonings; heat until cheese has melted. Remove soufflés from oven and serve immediately with hot cheese sauce.

Serves 2

PASTRY SHELL

1 cup all-purpose flour, sifted
1/2 teaspoon salt

1/4 pound butter
2 teaspoons ice water

Place flour and salt in a mixing bowl and cut in butter with a pastry blender until mixture resembles coarse meal. Mix in ice water. Form dough into a ball and chill. Roll out with rolling pin on a lightly floured board. Fit into a 9-inch pie pan, fluting the edges. If a prebaked crust is called for in the recipe prick all over with the tines of a fork or line the pie shell with aluminum foil and fill with dried beans or rice to hold in place. Bake in a preheated 400° oven for 10 minutes.

ZUCCHINI QUICHE

1-1/2 pounds zucchini, chopped
salt
1 prebaked 9-inch pastry shell,
  preceding
1 tablespoon fresh lemon juice
1/4 teaspoon salt

1/4 teaspoon pepper
3 tablespoons chopped parsley
3/4 cup grated Swiss cheese
3 eggs, beaten
1/2 cup heavy cream
1/2 cup plain yoghurt

Salt zucchini lightly and let stand in a colander 45 minutes to draw out moisture; pat dry. Prepare pastry shell. Combine zucchini with lemon juice, salt, pepper and parsley and place in pastry shell. Top with cheese. Mix eggs with cream and yoghurt and pour over zucchini mixture. Bake in a 350° oven for 35 minutes.
Serves 6

1 pound zucchini, thinly sliced
salt
1 prebaked 9-inch pastry shell,
   preceding
2 medium tomatoes, peeled, seeded
   and chopped
1/2 cup minced onion
1 garlic clove, minced
1 tablespoon chopped basil, tarragon
   or summer savory (or 1 teaspoon
   dried)

1/4 teaspoon salt
1/4 teaspoon pepper
1/2 cup grated Parmesan cheese
1-3/4 cups grated Gruyère cheese
1 cup milk or half-and-half
2 eggs, beaten
dash cayenne pepper

Salt zucchini lightly and let stand in a colander for 45 minutes to draw out moisture; pat dry. Prepare pastry shell and set aside. Combine zucchini, tomatoes, onion, garlic, seasoning and Parmesan cheese. Place 1 cup of the Gruyère cheese in the bottom of the pie shell and add zucchini mixture. Combine milk, eggs and cayenne and pour over top. Sprinkle with remaining Gruyère cheese. Bake in a 350° oven for 40 minutes.

Serves 6

ZUCCHINI-EGG CASSEROLE

2 pounds zucchini, thinly sliced
2 eggs, separated
1 teaspoon salt

1/4 cup minced parsley
1 pint (2 cups) sour cream
1/2 cup shredded Jarlsberg cheese

Cook zucchini in a small amount of boiling water until tender; drain and set aside. Beat egg yolks and stir in salt, parsley and sour cream. Beat egg whites until stiff, then fold into the sour cream mixture. Place half the cooked zucchini in a 2-quart buttered casserole and pour half the sour cream mixture over it. Layer the remaining squash in the casserole and pour over the remaining sour cream mixture. Sprinkle cheese over the top and bake in a 350° oven for 30 minutes.
Serves 4

ZUCCHINI AND EGGS

1 medium zucchini, sliced
1/4 cup olive oil
2 tablespoons butter
2 slices (1 ounce) prosciutto or
    salami, diced

3 eggs, beaten
1/2 teaspoon minced basil
salt and pepper to taste
1/4 cup grated Gruyère cheese

In a skillet sauté zucchini in oil and butter for 5 minutes. Add prosciutto or salami, stir and cook for 5 minutes. Mix basil, salt and pepper and half of the cheese with the beaten eggs. Add to the skillet, cover and continue cooking for 3 minutes. Season with salt and pepper. Sprinkle remaining cheese over the top and cook, covered, for 2 minutes.
Serves 2

main dishes with meat

SCALLOPS WITH ZUCCHINI

1 teaspoon salt
3/4 cup fine bread crumbs
1 egg
1 teaspoon water
1 tablespoon fresh lemon juice
1 pound bay scallops or quartered
    sea scallops

1 medium zucchini,
    cut in 1/4-inch slices
1/4 pound butter
hot buttered toast
1/4 cup chopped parsley
lemon wedges

Mix salt into bread crumbs. Beat egg with water and lemon juice. Roll scallops and zucchini in crumbs, dip in egg mixture, then dip again in crumbs. Heat butter in a skillet and cook scallops and squash until browned and tender, about 5 minutes. Serve on buttered toast. Sprinkle with parsley and garnish with lemon wedges.
Serves 4

GREEK-STYLE CHICKEN AND SQUASH

1 3-pound chicken, cut up
salt and pepper
2 tomatoes, peeled and chopped
1 small eggplant, cubed

4 small summer squash (zucchini,
　caserta or yellow), thinly sliced
1/2 pound mushrooms, quartered
2 garlic cloves, minced
1 teaspoon dried oregano

Sprinkle the chicken pieces with salt and pepper and place in a shallow buttered baking dish. Bake in a 450° oven until browned, about 15 minutes. Pour off any fat. Combine tomatoes, eggplant, squash, mushrooms, garlic and oregano and spoon over chicken. Bake, covered, for 45 minutes in a 350° oven.
Serves 4 to 6

CHICKEN WITH CROOKNECK SQUASH

1 3-pound chicken, cut up
4 tablespoons butter
2 garlic cloves, minced
salt and pepper to taste
1 cup chicken stock

1-1/2 pounds yellow crookneck,
　thickly sliced
1 egg, beaten
1/4 cup fresh lemon juice

Brown chicken in butter in a skillet. Add garlic, salt, pepper and chicken stock. Cover and simmer 20 minutes. Add squash and cook until squash is tender, about 5 minutes. Remove chicken and squash to a warm platter. Beat together egg and lemon juice, then add some of the pan juices slowly while beating. Return mixture to pan and heat on low until sauce is thickened. Pour over chicken to serve.
Serves 4 to 6

ZUCCHINI AND HAM CASSEROLE

1/2 cup cooked rice
4 small zucchini, chopped
1 leek, including some green tops,
   minced
1 cup ground cooked ham
2 eggs, beaten

1/2 teaspoon salt
1/4 teaspoon pepper
3/4 cup grated Swiss cheese
2 tablespoons butter, melted
1/4 cup soft whole-grain bread crumbs

Combine rice, zucchini, leek, ham, eggs, seasonings and 1/2 cup of the cheese. Put mixture in a buttered 1-1/2-quart casserole and sprinkle with remaining cheese, butter and bread crumbs. Bake in a 325° oven for 40 minutes.
Serves 4

MUSHROOMS, HAM AND ZUCCHINI

4 medium zucchini
1 onion, chopped
1/2 pound mushrooms, chopped
3 tablespoons butter
1 cup diced cooked ham

2 teaspoons fresh lemon juice
1/2 teaspoon salt
1/4 teaspoon pepper
dash cayenne pepper
2 tablespoons chopped parsley

Cut ends off zucchini, drop zucchini into boiling water and cook until almost tender. Cool, cut in half lengthwise and scoop out pulp, leaving a 1/4-inch thick shell. Sauté onion and mushrooms in butter. Add ham, seasonings and pulp and mix well. Place mixture in shells in a shallow buttered baking dish. Bake in a 350° oven for 25 minutes.
Serves 4 to 6

SUMMER SQUASH WITH LAMB STUFFING

4 medium zucchini or yellow
   straightneck
3/4 pound ground lamb, sautéed
1/4 cup ground almonds
1 tablespoon tomato paste
2 tablespoons chopped parsley

1/2 teaspoon salt
1/4 teaspoon pepper
1/2 teaspoon minced garlic
1/4 teaspoon dried rosemary
1 egg, beaten
1/4 cup grated Swiss cheese

Cut ends off squash, drop squash into boiling water and cook until almost tender, 8 to 10 minutes. Cool, cut squash in half lengthwise, scoop out pulp, leaving a 1/4-inch thick shell, and mash the pulp. Combine pulp with remaining ingredients, except cheese. Adjust seasonings. Divide mixture evenly in shells and place in a shallow buttered baking dish. Sprinkle cheese over top. Bake uncovered in a 350° oven for 30 minutes.
Serves 4

LAMB SHISH KEBAB WITH SUMMER SQUASH

1 pound lean lamb, cut in cubes
1 cup plain yoghurt
1/2 teaspoon pepper
1 garlic clove, minced
1 teaspoon dried thyme

3 yellow crookneck or straightneck,
   cut in thick slices
2 green bell peppers, cut in squares
12 pearl onions
olive oil or melted butter

Marinate meat in a mixture of the yoghurt, pepper, garlic and thyme for 1 hour. String lamb cubes and vegetables alternately on skewers. Brush with oil or melted butter. Broil until lamb is done to your liking, turning skewers occasionally. (If you like your lamb pink, parboil vegetables 3 to 5 minutes before broiling.)
Serves 4

LAMB CHOPS IN FOIL

8 loin lamb chops
salt and pepper
2 medium zucchini, trimmed,
 halved lengthwise, then crosswise
1/4 pound feta cheese or
 Swiss cheese, sliced

3 green onions, chopped
2 garlic cloves, minced
3 tablespoons fresh lemon juice
1/4 pound butter

Season lamb chops well on both sides with salt and pepper and put each on a large square of heavy foil. Place one piece of zucchini on each chop. Add slice of cheese, sprinkle with onions, garlic and lemon juice and dot with butter. Fold foil tightly at tops and sides. Bake in a 350° oven for 1 hour, or grill over charcoal, turning once, for 1 hour.
Serves 8

2 7-inch zucchini
3 tablespoons minced onion
1/2 garlic clove, minced
2 tablespoons olive oil
1/4 pound ground beef
3 tablespoons minced prosciutto
2 tablespoons minced parsley
pinch oregano

1/2 teaspoon salt
1/4 teaspoon pepper
1/3 cup grated Romano cheese
2 tablespoons bread crumbs
1 egg, beaten
1 cup Tomato Sauce, following
grated Romano cheese

Trim stem ends of zucchini and hollow them out with apple corer; be careful not to pierce skin. Save pulp. Drop zucchini shells in boiling salted water to cover for 5 minutes or until tender. Remove shells and let cool. Chop half the pulp very fine and squeeze out moisture on tea towel. Discard rest of pulp. Sauté onion and garlic in olive oil until onion is soft. Stir in ground beef, chopped zucchini pulp, prosciutto, parsley, oregano, salt and pepper. Cook until beef loses its pinkness. Remove from heat and stir in cheese, bread crumbs and egg. Stuff the shells with the mixture, using a teaspoon. Place shells in one layer on greased baking dish. Pour tomato sauce over and sprinkle with extra grated cheese. Bake at 350° for 25 minutes.
Serves 2

3 medium zucchini
1 pound ground round
1/2 cup sourdough French bread crumbs
1/3 cup grated Parmesan cheese
1 egg, beaten
1 teaspoon salt
1/4 teaspoon pepper
3 tablespoons minced parsley

Tomato Sauce
1 garlic clove, minced
2 tablespoons olive oil
3 ripe tomatoes, peeled,
    seeded and chopped
1-1/2 tablespoons chopped basil
salt and freshly ground pepper

Trim ends from zucchini and drop zucchini into boiling water; cook until barely tender, about 7 minutes. Cool, cut in half lengthwise and scoop out pulp, leaving a 1/2-inch thick shell. Mix together pulp, beef, bread crumbs, cheese and egg. Add salt, pepper and parsley. Fill shells with mixture and place in a shallow baking dish. Bake in a 350° oven for 45 minutes. Just before removing the stuffed zucchini from the oven, prepare the tomato sauce. Sauté garlic in olive oil in a skillet, add tomatoes and basil and stir over medium heat 5 to 8 minutes. Add salt and pepper to taste. Place zucchini on a platter and spoon the tomato sauce over top.
Serves 4 to 6

Variations
• Substitute 1 cup béchamel or mornay sauce for the tomato sauce.
• A variety of cheeses may be used in place of the Parmesan, such as feta, Cheddar or Romano.
• To the ground round stuffing add 1/4 to 1/2 teaspoon each ground cumin and dried oregano and substitute Monterey jack for the Parmesan. Add 1 small fresh green chili pepper, seeded and minced, to the tomato sauce. Sprinkle 2 tablespoons shredded Monterey jack over top just before serving.

STUFFED WINTER SQUASH

Acorn and Delicata squash take to a variety of stuffings. The general procedure is to cut the squash in half, scrape out seeds and place, cut side down, in a shallow baking dish with hot water to 1/4 inch. You may bake it rapidly in a hot oven (30 minutes at 400°) or, to bring out more flavor, for 45 minutes in a 350° oven. Fill with any precooked stuffing of your choice and bake another 10 minutes. Suggested stuffings: creamed chicken or crab with almonds, ham and creamed mushrooms or asparagus, curried shrimp.

LAMB-STUFFED ACORN SQUASH

2 acorn squash, cut in half with
   seeds and fibers removed
1/2 pound ground lean lamb
1 tablespoon olive oil
1 onion, minced
1 cup cooked bulghur
1 tablespoon minced mint leaves
   (or 1 teaspoon dried mint)

salt and pepper to taste
1/4 teaspoon dried rosemary
1/4 teaspoon ground cinnamon
1/4 cup white raisins
1 tablespoon butter, at room
   temperature

Place acorn squash cut side down in a shallow baking dish with hot water to 1/4 inch and bake 20 minutes in a 400° oven. While squash is cooking, brown meat in olive oil, add remaining ingredients, except butter, and simmer 20 minutes. Rub cut surface of squash with butter. Mound one-fourth of meat mixture in each squash. Bake in a 350° oven for 45 minutes.
Serves 4

SQUASH-SAUSAGE BAKE

2 medium-to-large acorn squash, cut
   in half with seeds and fibers removed
1 pound bulk pork sausage
1/2 cup chopped onion
3/4 cup cubed French bread
1 tablespoon butter

1/4 teaspoon dried sage
1 8-ounce can crushed pineapple,
   drained
salt

Place acorn squash cut side down in a shallow baking dish with hot water to 1/4 inch and bake 20 minutes in a 400° oven. While squash is cooking, brown sausage in a hot skillet, then add the onion and sauté until onion is translucent. Sauté bread cubes in butter until lightly toasted. Toss with dried sage. Drain excess fat from the sausage and add pineapple and 1/2 cup of the toasted bread cubes, reserving the remaining cubes. Sprinkle cut side of each squash with salt and fill with one-fourth of meat mixture. Crush reserved bread cubes and sprinkle over top. Bake in a 350° oven for 25 minutes.
Serves 4

ACORN SQUASH WITH GROUND BEEF FILLING

2 medium-to-large acorn squash, cut in
    half with seeds and fibers removed
3/4 pound ground beef
2 tablespoons chopped onion
1/2 teaspoon salt

1 teaspoon curry powder
1/2 cup milk
1 egg, lightly beaten
1/2 cup bread crumbs
1/2 cup grated Monterey jack cheese

Place squash cut side down in a shallow baking dish with hot water to 1/4 inch. Bake
for 15 minutes in a 425° oven. Mix ground beef with all other ingredients except
cheese. Fill shells with meat mixture. Bake 45 minutes at 375°. Sprinkle with cheese
and return to oven until cheese is melted.
Serves 4

ZUCCHINI WITH MEATBALLS

1/2 cup bread crumbs (leftover
    garlic bread is good)
1/2 cup milk
1/2 pound ground pork
1/2 pound ground veal
1/2 teaspoon salt
2 pounds zucchini, cubed

1 large onion, chopped
1 garlic clove, minced
2 tablespoons butter
2 tomatoes, peeled and chopped
2 cups freshly grated corn kernels
salt and pepper to taste
1/4 cup grated Parmesan cheese

Soak the bread crumbs in the milk. Add meats and salt. Form into meatballs about the size of a marble. Brown meatballs in a skillet, remove and set aside. In the same pan sauté zucchini, onion and garlic in butter until onion is translucent. Add tomatoes and corn and season to taste. Add meatballs, put in a 2-quart buttered casserole and bake in a 350° oven for 20 minutes. Sprinkle Parmesan cheese on top and bake until cheese is melted.
Serves 6

SAUSAGE AND ZUCCHINI

4 medium zucchini
1/4 cup chopped onion
1 garlic clove, minced
1/2 pound bulk pork sausage
1/2 cup whole-grain cracker crumbs

1 egg, beaten
1/4 teaspoon salt
pinch each dried thyme and pepper
2/3 cup grated Parmesan cheese

Cut off ends of zucchini, drop zucchini into boiling water and cook until almost tender, about 8 to 10 minutes. Cool, cut zucchini in half lengthwise, scoop out pulp leaving a 1/2-inch thick shell, and mash pulp. Sauté onion, garlic and sausage until sausage is browned, draining off extra fat. Combine with mashed pulp. Add all remaining ingredients, reserving 4 tablespoons of the cheese. Divide mixture evenly in shells and place in shallow buttered baking dish. Sprinkle with reserved cheese. Bake in a 350° oven for 30 minutes.
Serves 4

ZUCCHINI AND EGGPLANT LASAGNE

1/2 pound ground veal or lamb
1 onion, chopped
1/2 teaspoon dried thyme
1/2 teaspoon salt
1/4 teaspoon pepper
2 cups peeled and chopped tomatoes

1 eggplant, cut in lengthwise
   slices 1/2 inch thick
2 medium zucchini, sliced
   lengthwise 1/2 inch thick
1/4 cup olive oil
1/2 pound mozzarella cheese,
   thinly sliced

In a skillet brown ground veal or lamb with the chopped onion. Add thyme, salt, pepper and tomatoes and simmer for 10 minutes. While meat sauce is simmering, in another skillet sauté eggplant and zucchini slices in oil until brown. In a shallow oiled baking dish, make a layer of eggplant, top with a layer of zucchini and cover with half of the meat sauce. Repeat layers, ending with meat sauce. Top with cheese. Bake in a 350° oven for 40 minutes.
Serves 4 to 6

ZUCCHINI GARDEN CASSEROLE

4 small zucchini, sliced
4 medium tomatoes, peeled and sliced
2/3 cup rice
1-1/2 pounds ground veal
2 tablespoons chopped parsley
1/4 cup minced green bell pepper

1/4 cup minced onion
1 teaspoon salt
1/2 teaspoon pepper
1 cup grated mozzarella cheese
1 cup chicken stock

Layer half the zucchini slices in a shallow buttered baking dish, then half the tomato slices. Combine rice, veal, parsley, green pepper, onion, salt, pepper, cheese and chicken stock. Add to casserole. Layer remaining zucchini and tomato slices over mixture. Bake, covered, in a 350° oven for 45 minutes to 1 hour, or until rice and vegetables are tender.
Serves 6

KIDNEY-SUMMER SQUASH CASSEROLE

3 veal kidneys, or
6 lamb kidneys
1/2 teaspoon paprika
1 cup chicken or vegetable stock, boiling
2 tablespoons butter
1/2 pound mushrooms, sliced
1-1/2 cups diced zucchini or
   other summer squash

2 tablespoons minced onion
1 tablespoon minced parsley
2 tablespoons flour
1/4 cup dry sherry or white wine
1/2 teaspoon salt
1/4 teaspoon freshly ground pepper
hot toast

Trim fat and white tissue from kidneys and dice. Dust with paprika. Drop in boiling stock and simmer 3 minutes. Remove, drain and place in heated casserole. Reserve stock and keep hot. Melt butter in a skillet and sauté mushrooms, squash, onion and parsley, stirring, about 2 minutes. Stir in flour, then hot stock. Bring to a boil, and cook and stir about 2 minutes or until thickened. Add sherry and seasonings. Pour over kidneys, cover casserole, and bake at 350° for 20 minutes. Serve on hot toast.
Serves 4

1 4-pound spaghetti squash

Meat Sauce
1 garlic clove, minced
1/2 cup chopped onion
1/2 cup olive oil
1 pound ground beef, or
1/2 pound each ground beef and
ground veal
2 cups peeled and chopped
Italian plum tomatoes

1/2 cup tomato paste
1/2 cup beef stock
1-1/2 teaspoons salt
1/4 teaspoon pepper
1/4 teaspoon dried basil
1 bay leaf
5 dried Italian mushrooms, soaked
in warm water to soften, drained and
slivered (optional)

Split squash and place, cut side down, in a flat baking pan with hot water to 1/4 inch. Bake at 350° for 45 minutes. Turn and bake 30 minutes more.

While squash is baking make sauce. Sauté garlic and onion in olive oil in a large skillet until onion is translucent; add meat and brown lightly. Drain off fat, add remaining ingredients and simmer uncovered for 1 hour. Scoop seeds and fiber from baked squash, and loosen the flesh with a fork. Pour half the sauce over squash and serve the remainder on the side.

Serves 6 to 8

sweets & breads

ZUCCHINI COOKIES

1-1/2 cups firmly packed brown sugar
1 cup shortening
2 eggs
3/4 cup shredded zucchini
2 cups all-purpose flour
1 teaspoon baking soda
1/2 teaspoon baking powder

1/2 teaspoon salt
1/2 teaspoon ground cinnamon
1/2 teaspoon ground nutmeg
1 cup rolled oats
1 cup uncooked semolina
1 cup chopped toasted almonds
1/2 teaspoon almond extract

Cream brown sugar and shortening; add eggs and beat until light. Stir in zucchini. Sift together flour, baking soda, baking powder, salt, cinnamon and nutmeg and add to egg mixture. Stir in oats, semolina, nuts and almond extract. Drop by teaspoonfuls onto greased cookie sheets. Bake in a 375° oven for 10 to 12 minutes or until lightly browned.
Makes about 6 dozen cookies

ELENA'S BUTTERNUT PIE

Pastry Dough
1 cup whole wheat flour
1 cup rolled oats
1/4 cup wheat germ
1/2 teaspoon salt
1/4 cup corn oil
about 1/2 cup ice water

Filling
3 tablespoons honey
1 tablespoon butter
3 tablespoons dark rum (optional)
1/2 teaspoon ground cinnamon
1/2 teaspoon ground allspice
3 cups hot, cooked puréed butternut
    squash (about a 2-1/2 pound squash)
1/2 cup ground almonds, hazelnuts or
    walnuts

Combine all ingredients for pastry except ice water. Add enough ice water to make a dough consistency. Press with fingers into a 9-inch pie pan. Mix honey, butter, optional rum and spices into squash. Pour filling into unbaked pie crust, top with ground nuts and bake at 375° for 45 minutes.

BUTTERNUT SQUASH PIE

1 cup cooked and puréed butternut
   squash
1/2 cup firmly packed brown sugar
2 eggs, beaten
1/2 cup heavy cream
1/2 teaspoon ground cinnamon

1/4 teaspoon salt
1/8 teaspoon ground ginger
1/8 teaspoon ground nutmeg
1 unbaked 9-inch pastry shell, page 60
Pecan Topping, following (optional)

Combine squash, brown sugar, eggs, cream, cinnamon, salt, ginger and nutmeg in a bowl and mix well. Pour into pastry shell and bake in a 375° oven for 30 to 35 minutes or until a knife inserted in the center comes out clean. If desired, add Pecan Topping when pie is cool.

Pecan Topping Cream together 1/2 cup firmly packed brown sugar and 4 tablespoons softened butter. Stir in 1/2 cup chopped pecans and spoon over top of pie. Place under a broiler for 2 minutes or until bubbly.

SQUASH MUFFINS

1-1/2 cups all-purpose flour
1/2 cup sugar
2 teaspoons baking powder
3/4 teaspoon salt
1/2 teaspoon ground cinnamon
1/2 teaspoon ground nutmeg

4 tablespoons butter
1/2 cup dried currants
1 egg, beaten
1/2 cup cooked and puréed winter
  squash
1/2 cup milk
1 tablespoon sugar

Sift together flour, sugar, baking powder, salt, cinnamon and nutmeg. Cut in butter with a pastry blender and add currants. Combine egg with squash and milk and add to flour mixture. Mix just enough to combine. Fill greased muffin tins two-thirds full. Sprinkle 1/4 teaspoon sugar over each muffin. Bake in a 400° oven for 18 to 20 minutes; serve hot.
Makes 12 muffins

1-1/2 cups all-purpose flour
2 teaspoons baking powder
1/2 teaspoon baking soda
1/2 teaspoon salt
1/4 teaspoon ground nutmeg
1/2 teaspoon ground cinnamon
1 cup sugar

1/2 cup corn oil
2 eggs, beaten
1 cup grated zucchini
1 teaspoon grated lemon peel
1/2 cup fresh orange juice
1/2 cup chopped pecans or walnuts

Sift together flour, baking powder, baking soda, salt, nutmeg and cinnamon. Mix together sugar, oil, eggs and zucchini. Add dry ingredients to egg mixture, beating well. Add lemon peel, orange juice and nuts. Pour into a buttered loaf pan and bake in a 350° oven for 55 minutes or until a toothpick inserted in the center comes out clean. Cool on a rack for 10 minutes before removing loaf.
Makes 1 loaf

PEAR-ZUCCHINI BREAD

2 cups all-purpose flour
2 teaspoons baking soda
1 teaspoon ground allspice
1/4 teaspoon ground nutmeg
1/2 teaspoon salt
2 eggs, beaten
1 cup firmly packed brown sugar

1 cup granulated sugar
3/4 cup corn oil
2 teaspoons vanilla extract
2 cups grated zucchini
1 cup raisins
1 cup chopped almonds or walnuts
2 cups peeled and diced pears

Sift together flour, baking soda, allspice, nutmeg and salt. Mix together the eggs, brown and granulated sugar, corn oil and vanilla extract. Add dry ingredients to egg mixture, then mix in zucchini, raisins and nuts; add pears last. Pour mixture into 2 well-greased and floured loaf pans and bake at 350° for 40 to 50 minutes or until a toothpick inserted in the center comes out clean. Remove from oven and let cool on a rack for 10 minutes before removing from pans.
Makes 2 loaves

1/4 cup safflower oil
4 tablespoons butter, at room
   temperature
1/2 cup firmly packed brown
   sugar
1/2 cup granulated sugar
2 cups all-purpose flour
2 tablespoons cornstarch

1 tablespoon baking powder
2/3 cup milk
1/2 teaspoon vanilla extract
1 teaspoon grated orange peel
1 cup finely chopped zucchini
3 egg whites
Lemon Frosting, following

Mix together oil and butter; add brown and granulated sugars. Beat until fluffy. Mix flour, cornstarch and baking powder together. Add alternately with milk to the butter and sugar mixture, stirring until smooth. Add vanilla extract, orange peel and zucchini. Beat egg whites until stiff and fold into cake mixture. Spoon in 2 buttered and floured 9-inch cake pans and bake at 375° for 25 minutes. Cool on a rack. Ice with Lemon Frosting, following.

Lemon Frosting Combine 2 cups confectioners' sugar, 1 tablespoon melted butter, 1 tablespoon grated lemon rind and 1/4 cup fresh lemon juice in the top of a double boiler; stir. Place pan over hot water for 15 minutes, stirring constantly. Cool and beat icing until it is of spreading consistency. Place frosting between cake layers and frost top.

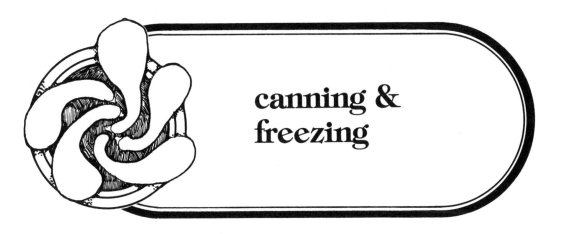

canning & freezing

GENERAL PROCEDURES FOR CANNING

All equipment and utensils (except canning lids with sealing compound attached) must be first washed in hot soapy water, then sterilized by boiling in water to cover for 20 minutes, and left in the hot water until used. Use nonmetal cups and wooden spoons. A wide-mouthed funnel is handy for filling jars. Tongs or jar lifters are necessary for removing jars from the kettle. Preserving kettles should be stainless steel or enamel—never copper, brass, galvanized steel or iron.

Never use jars or lids from commercially canned food, such as mayonnaise, as they are designed for special packing machines, not home use.

Always follow manufacturer's instructions for canning jars and lids. Jars should be tempered glass. Be sure they are free from cracks and chips and completely clean.

If you use metal lids and ring bands for closures, only new, unused lids are safe—once used, the sealing compound loses effectiveness. But the ring bands may be reused if they are nonrusted and in good condition. If using this type of closure, wipe jar rim with a *clean* cloth after squash is packed in jar; place lid on jar with sealing compound next to glass; screw band on tight; do not tighten farther after taking jar from canner; and never turn jars upside down. Leave jars undisturbed for 12 hours.

If you use glass lids with rubber rings, be sure rings are new. Stretch wet rubber ring slightly to fit it on ledge of jar after jar is filled; push wire bail on top of lid so it fits into the groove; leave short wire up during processing. After jars are processed push short wire down to complete seal.

The scarcer zinc caps with porcelain linings and rubber rings are also fine for canning squash. Be sure caps are not cracked or bent and will give good closure. Fit the wet ring on jar shoulder (avoiding undue stretching); fill jar; wipe ring and jar rim clean; screw cap down firmly and turn it back 1/4 inch. When you take jar from canner, screw cap down tight to complete seal. Do not invert. If properly sealed, lids will make a "tinging" sound when struck; a dull sound is indicative of improper closure.

Once the jars have been processed they should be left undisturbed for 12 hours. Then store in a cool place, 45° to 60°F, out of any drafts.

Both summer and winter squash may easily be preserved in glass jars. Always process in a steam pressure canner to avoid danger of botulism, which is a much greater hazard with vegetables and other low-acid foods than with fruits, tomatoes, pickles and relishes. *Never* process vegetables in a regular canning kettle.

Please note: Because of the danger of botulism, squash and all other non-acid home-canned vegetables should be boiled in an open pan, and stirred frequently, for 15 minutes before tasting or serving.

CANNING SUMMER SQUASH
Zucchini, cymlings, young yellow crooknecks, straightnecks, caserta, etc., may be canned by either of two methods: hot pack (recommended by authorities as the surer, safer way for these low-acid vegetables) or raw pack. The latter may be preferable for zucchini, because it takes very little cooking to reduce zucchini to a mushy consistency.

84

Hot pack method Wash squash; do not peel. Cut in 1/2-inch thick slices. Halve or quarter if necessary to make pieces that will fit easily in jar. Place squash in kettle, cover with water, bring to boil and keep squash just at boiling point. Pack loosely in hot sterilized jars. Add 1 teaspoon salt per quart, 1/2 teaspoon per pint, if desired. (The salt isn't essential for preserving, if you are concerned about salt-free diets.) Fill jar with water in which squash was cooked, or boiling water if you need more, to within 1/2 inch of top, to permit contents to expand when heated and drive air out of the jar during processing. Put on cap and adjust. Process in pressure canner at 10 pounds pressure for 30 minutes (pints) or 40 minutes (quarts).

Raw pack method Wash squash; do not peel. Cut in pieces as above. Pack tightly into hot sterilized jars to within 1/2 inch of top. Add 1 teaspoon salt per quart, 1/2 teaspoon per pint, if desired. Fill to within 1/2 inch of top of jar with boiling water. Put on cap; adjust. Process in pressure canner at 10 pounds pressure for 25 minutes (pints), or 30 minutes (quarts).

Yield By either method, a half-bushel (20 pounds) of squash should give you from 8 to 10 quarts. For smaller quantities, allow 1-1/2 pounds of squash per quart.

CANNING WINTER SQUASH

Hubbard, acorn, banana, etc. take a longer processing time because heat penetrates such starchy, low-acid foods more slowly and it takes longer to pressure seal the jar.

Peel squash, remove seeds and cut in 1-inch cubes. Steam or boil until tender (about 25 minutes). Drain, put through sieve or food mill or mash thoroughly. Simmer until heated through, stirring. Season, if desired. Pack in clean jars to within 1/2 inch of top. Put on cap, adjust, and process in pressure canner at 10 pounds pressure for 1 hour (pints), or 1 hour 20 minutes (quarts).

Yield Ten pounds of winter squash will yield about 3 quarts; or allow about 2 to 3 pounds per quart.

GENERAL PROCEDURES FOR FREEZING

Use only the highest grade of vegetables for freezing. They should be processed as soon after harvest as possible.

Vegetables that are frozen are closer in taste, texture and appearance to fresh vegetables than are canned vegetables. And freezing preserves the nutritive value.

Freezing is easy and fast. Your freezer should maintain 0°F. The small compartment or ice-cube section in your refrigerator, with a range of 15° to 20°F, should be used only for short-term freezing.

Aluminum containers that can go from freezer to oven may be used for dishes that only need to be heated through.

FREEZING SUMMER SQUASH

Choose young squash with small seeds and a tender rind. Wash thoroughly. Cut in 1/2-inch slices. Immerse wire basket or cheesecloth bag containing squash in boiling water for 2 to 3 minutes. Use a gallon of water per pint of vegetable. Start timing the moment you place the squash in the water. The heat stops the natural enzyme action that would otherwise cause undesirable changes when squash is frozen.

Remove from boiling water, cool immediately in cold water and drain. Pack in freezer containers, leaving 1/2-inch headroom. Seal, label (including date) and freeze. One to 1-1/4 pounds summer squash will yield 1 pint.

Grated zucchini for breads may be grated and frozen without blanching.

Freezing containers should be vapor-, air- and moisture-proof. Use plastic boxes with tight-fitting lids, glass jars with matching lids, plastic bags with seal tops or aluminum freezer containers. No container will protect frozen foods properly unless its seal is tight enough to prevent air from entering or moisture from escaping. Containers should be labeled and dated.

Squash may be cooked from the frozen state. Cook frozen squash in small amount of water, but cook only half as long as if it were fresh.

FREEZING WINTER SQUASH PURÉE

Cut squash in pieces and remove seeds. Cook in boiling water until tender. Cool, then peel off skin. Put squash through a food mill, sieve or potato ricer. Pack in freezer containers, leaving 1/2-inch headroom. Seal, label (including date) and freeze. Three pounds of winter squash will yield 2 pints.

If desired, seasonings such as salt, pepper, butter or nutmeg may be added to the squash before freezing.

FREEZING SUMMER SQUASH PURÉE

Scrub summer squash, trim ends and cut squash in thin slices. Cook in a small amount of boiling water until tender, about 8 to 10 minutes. Put squash through a food mill, sieve or potato ricer. Cool, then pack in freezer containers, leaving 1/2-inch headroom. Seal, label (including date) and freeze. One to 1-1/4 pounds of summer squash will yield 1 pint.

If you wish to prepare frozen summer squash purée that can go from freezer to oven, use the following method.

1 large onion, thinly sliced	1 garlic clove, crushed
3 tablespoons butter	1/2 teaspoon salt
3 pounds summer squash, thinly sliced	1/4 teaspoon pepper
1 green bell pepper, cut in julienne	1/4 cup chopped parsley, basil or
2 tablespoons water	tarragon (optional)

In a large kettle, sauté onion in butter until onion is translucent. Add squash, green pepper, water, garlic, salt and pepper and cook over medium heat for 12 to 15 minutes. Remove from heat and add parsley, basil or tarragon, if desired. Whirl vegetables (with cooking liquid) in a blender 1/2 cup at a time until all the squash is blender-puréed. Cool, then pack in aluminum freezer containers. Seal, label (including date) and freeze.

pickles
relishes &
preserves

The procedure for pickling squash is the same as for cucumbers and other vegetables. (See general procedures for canning, page 83.) You may use a water-bath canner instead of a pressure canner for pickles, since their higher acid content means they don't require such high temperatures during processing. Following are a few pointers on pickling squash.

Salt Use pure granulated salt (either pickling or coarse salt, as specified in the recipe). Do not use iodized salt as it causes pickles to darken.

Vinegar Cider vinegar or distilled white vinegar of 4 to 6 percent acidity may be used. Never dilute vinegar unless recipe calls for it. Instead use more sugar for a less tart pickle.

Water If you live in a hard water area, you may prefer to use distilled water in pickling, as hard water will darken pickles.

Filling jars First wash, then sterilize jars by boiling in water to cover for 20 minutes. All utensils should be sterilized as well. Keep jars, lids and utensils in the hot water until they are used. Pour hot pickles into sterilized jars. Avoid packing so tightly that pickle brine cannot cover pickles. Be sure to leave 1/2-inch headroom at the top to permit expansion during processing. Wipe jars clean after filling, especially around the rim threads.

Water-bath processing If you use this method, you will need a large kettle that can hold jars with space for 1 to 2 inches of water above jar tops, and a 2-inch space between the jars. The kettle should have a tight-fitting cover. You will also need a rack to set the jars on which will fit in the bottom of the kettle. Lower the filled, sealed jars into the kettle which is half-filled with boiling water. Add more boiling water to cover the jars by 2 inches, directing the flow of water down the sides of the kettle rather than onto the jar tops. When the water comes to a rolling boil, cover the kettle and process the recommended time. Remove jars from the kettle by using tongs or a specially designed jar lifter and by grasping the jar itself, not the lid. Cool on a rack, making sure the jars do not touch and also that they are not in a draft which could cause them to crack. If properly sealed, lids will make a "tinging" sound when struck; a dull sound means improper closure.

Check jars carefully before storage. If there is any sign of leakage, bulging lids, etc. use contents at once or reprocess using a new pickling solution. If after storage you are at all doubtful about the safety of eating the contents, discard immediately. Do not test the contents by tasting.

Store pickles in a cool, dark place. Most pickles are best if stored for at least 1 month before eating.

QUICK SUMMER SQUASH PICKLE

1 small yellow crookneck or
   straightneck squash

1 small zucchini
2 cups dill pickle juice

Cut unpeeled squash in sticks, 3 to 4 inches long. Bring to boil in pickle juice, lower heat and simmer 3 to 5 minutes, until crisp-tender. Remove from heat at once and chill in liquid 24 hours before serving. Keeps well in refrigerator.
Makes about 1-1/2 pints

HOT ZUCCHINI PICKLE

12 cups sliced zucchini (1/4-inch thick
   and quartered, if large)
3 dozen pearl onions, peeled and
   left whole
1/2 cup pickling salt
1 quart cider vinegar
2 cups sugar

2 teaspoons celery seed
2 teaspoons dry mustard
2 teaspoons mustard seed
2 teaspoons ground turmeric
2 garlic cloves, peeled, blanched
     for 1 minute and then minced

Combine zucchini and onions in a large bowl, sprinkle with salt, cover with cold water and let stand 1 hour. Drain and rinse. Combine remaining ingredients in a large kettle, bring to a boil and pour over zucchini and onions. Let stand 1 hour. Place mixture in kettle, bring to a boil and cook 3 minutes. Put into sterilized jars and seal immediately. Process 15 minutes in a boiling water bath.
Makes about 2 quarts

REFRIGERATOR ZUCCHINI PICKLES

1/2 cup cider vinegar
1/2 cup water
1/3 cup sugar
3 tablespoons sliced green onion tops

1 garlic clove, crushed
1/2 teaspoon salt
1/2 teaspoon celery seed
3 medium zucchini, thinly sliced

Place all ingredients except zucchini in a quart jar and shake. Add zucchini and shake jar again. Refrigerate overnight. Drain to serve.

    This zucchini pickle should be used within a few days as it is not sterilized and sealed.
Makes about 1 quart

ZUCCHINI PICKLE RELISH I

5 pounds zucchini, chopped
1 pound white onions, chopped
5 tablespoons pickling salt
2-1/4 cups cider vinegar
1-1/4 cups sugar

1 teaspoon dry mustard
2 teaspoons celery seed
1/2 teaspoon pepper
1/2 teaspoon ground cinnamon
1/2 teaspoon ground nutmeg

Combine squash and onions in a large bowl, sprinkle with salt, cover with cold water and let stand overnight. Drain, rinse and place in a large kettle. Add all remaining ingredients, bring to a boil and simmer 5 minutes. Put into sterilized pint jars and seal immediately. Process 15 minutes in a boiling water bath.
Makes about 5 pints

ZUCCHINI PICKLE RELISH II

10 medium zucchini, chopped
4 medium onions, chopped
2 green bell peppers, seeded and
   chopped
2 sweet red peppers, seeded and
   chopped
1/2 cup pickling salt

4 cups sugar
2 cups cider vinegar
1 teaspoon ground turmeric
1 teaspoon celery salt
1 teaspoon curry powder
1/2 teaspoon pepper

Combine zucchini, onions and peppers in a large bowl, sprinkle with salt and cover with cold water. Let stand overnight. Drain and rinse and place in a large kettle. Add all remaining ingredients, bring to a boil and simmer 10 minutes. Put into sterilized pint jars and seal immediately. Process 15 minutes in a boiling water bath.
Makes about 5 pints

ZUCCHINI RELISH FOR MEAT

10 medium zucchini, chopped
2 large onions, chopped
1 green bell pepper, chopped
1/4 cup pickling salt
1/2 cup sugar

1 cup white wine vinegar
1 teaspoon dry mustard
1 teaspoon celery seed
1 4-ounce jar pimientos, chopped

Combine zucchini, onions and pepper in a large bowl, sprinkle with salt, cover with cold water and let stand overnight. Drain, rinse, place in a large kettle and add remaining ingredients and bring to a boil, stirring. Reduce heat to simmer and cook, uncovered, until mixture is reduced to 1-1/2 quarts. Put into sterilized jars and seal immediately. Process 15 minutes in a boiling water bath.
Makes about 5 pints

FRESH VEGETABLE RELISH FOR MEAT

1 medium tomato, peeled and chopped
1 medium green bell pepper, chopped
1 medium zucchini, chopped
1 medium onion, chopped
1 celery stalk, chopped

1/2 cucumber, peeled and chopped
1/4 cup sugar
1/4 cup cider vinegar
salt and pepper to taste

Combine all ingredients and stir until well blended. Cover and refrigerate overnight. To serve, strain off and discard liquid.
Serves 4

ZUCCHINI MARMALADE

2 pounds small, young zucchini, thinly sliced (about 6 cups)
juice of 2 lemons
peel of the lemons, cut in thin strips
1 13-1/2 ounce can crushed pineapple, drained, or

1-1/2 cups chopped fresh pineapple
1 1-3/4-ounce package powdered pectin
5 cups sugar
2 tablespoons chopped crystallized ginger

Place the zucchini in a large kettle. Add lemon juice, peel and pineapple. Bring to a boil and simmer over low heat, uncovered, until tender, about 20 minutes. Add pectin, bring to a full boil, add sugar and ginger and boil 1 to 2 minutes. Fill sterilized jars and seal immediately. Process 15 minutes in a boiling water bath.
Makes about 5 pints

SQUASH BUTTER

6 pounds winter squash, such as acorn or Hubbard
3 cups firmly packed brown sugar
1/4 cup fresh lemon juice

1 teaspoon grated lemon peel
1 teaspoon salt
2 teaspoons ground cinnamon
1/4 teaspoon ground nutmeg

Cut squash in half (if using acorn) or in pieces (if using Hubbard). Remove seeds and cook covered in a small amount of boiling water in a large kettle until tender, about 45 minutes. Drain and scoop out pulp. Whip pulp with electric mixer until smooth.

Place pulp (you should have 6 cups) and remaining ingredients in a large kettle. Cook and stir until mixture begins to boil. Fill sterilized jars and seal immediately. Process 15 minutes in a boiling water bath.
Makes about 4 pints

index to recipes

94

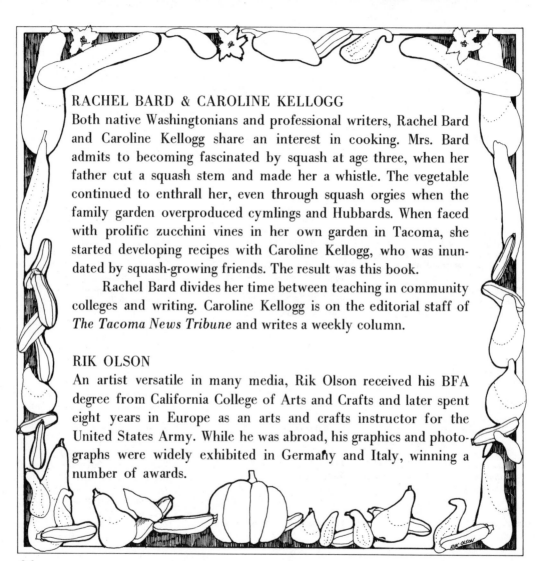

RACHEL BARD & CAROLINE KELLOGG

Both native Washingtonians and professional writers, Rachel Bard and Caroline Kellogg share an interest in cooking. Mrs. Bard admits to becoming fascinated by squash at age three, when her father cut a squash stem and made her a whistle. The vegetable continued to enthrall her, even through squash orgies when the family garden overproduced cymlings and Hubbards. When faced with prolific zucchini vines in her own garden in Tacoma, she started developing recipes with Caroline Kellogg, who was inundated by squash-growing friends. The result was this book.

Rachel Bard divides her time between teaching in community colleges and writing. Caroline Kellogg is on the editorial staff of *The Tacoma News Tribune* and writes a weekly column.

RIK OLSON

An artist versatile in many media, Rik Olson received his BFA degree from California College of Arts and Crafts and later spent eight years in Europe as an arts and crafts instructor for the United States Army. While he was abroad, his graphics and photographs were widely exhibited in Germany and Italy, winning a number of awards.